Cheap Talk with the Frugal Friends

OVER 500 TIPS, TRICKS, AND CREATIVE IDEAS FOR SAVING MONEY

by Angie Zalewski and Deana Ricks

STARBURST PUBLISHERS

P.O. Box 4123, Lancaster, PA 17604
www.starburstpublishers.com

To schedule author appearances, contact:

Author Appearances
Frugal Family Network, Inc.
P.O. Box 92731
Austin, TX 78709
Phone: 512-891-9031
email: Angie@frugalfamilynetwork.com

CREDITS:
Cover design by David Marty Design
Text design and composition by Booksetters
Illustrations by Pattie Ferrick and Suzanne King

All information published in this book is taken from our personal experiences, tips from readers throughout the country, or from the most reliable sources possible. These tips are given as information only, and all readers should practice common sense when using this information. They are not intended as a substitute for professional advice. The authors, publisher, and Frugal Family Network, Inc. assume no responsibility for any consequences suffered during or as a result of following this information.

First printing, September 2001
ISBN: 1-892016-58-3
Library of Congress Catalog Number: 2001088303
Printed in USA

Contents

Acknowledgments

We dedicate this book to God for bringing us together "for such a time as this."

Thanks to our husbands, Tom Zalewski for being Mr. Mom and Joe Ricks for being POD (Parent On Duty) during the writing of this book. Thanks to our precious children, Katie and Alex Ricks, and Timothy and Adam Zalewski, who make frugality fun. We honor our parents, Loretta and the late LeRoy Nietfeld, and Don and Glenda Williams, for their inspiration. And our siblings Denise Williams Wash, Diana Hulme, Betty Lautenschlager, Gary Nietfeld, and Jerry Nietfeld for their encouragement.

Special thanks to our dear friend Donna Ledbetter, who offered emotional and physical support. Thanks for saying you are proud of us.

Gratefulness also to Jeana Hensley, Dolores Pickens, Dr. Matthew Ricks, Chris Tressler, Joe Zalewski, Donald Nietfeld, and Lin Harris for your input and help with this book. Thanks also to Barbara Ledbetter, Evelyn Davison, Barbara Rosenkotter, Pattie Ferrick, Suzanne King, and from KIXL radio, Gene Bender and Ed Sossen, and the folks at KEYE-42, TV.

And special gratitude to our mothers-in-law, Pat Zalewski and Pauline Ricks, who were the first two people to subscribe to our newsletter. We hope we will be equally supportive mothers-in-law when our turn comes. Thanks also to our friends who answered many "What do you think of this?" questions, especially Circle Fellowship Homeschool Mom's group.

Introduction

Deana and I met in 1993 and shared a passion for our kids, careers as homemakers, and the frugality that made our one-income families possible. Our reputation as "sisters of savings" grew. In 1997, our church was hosting a parenting conference and the director asked us to put together a workshop on family budgeting. "Stretching the Family Dollar or How I Bought a Minivan by Washing out Baggies," was the name of that first presentation. The workshop was a hit, and soon other churches asked us to speak. After our presentations folks wanted to take home a piece of what they had just learned—something to provide ongoing encouragement and practical ideas as they began a frugal life.

So with prayerful consideration, we started the Frugal Family Network. Our first task was to put together a newsletter. We announced it to the local media and, lo and behold, if they didn't ask us to come on their shows. This led to a weekly frugal segment on our local CBS station. We know God has a sense of humor to put us on television! The television gig led to radio, which led to a website, which led to more workshops, which led to the book you're now holding.

It would be easy to look at us now and assume we've been thrifty all our lives. But we haven't, or at least one of us hasn't. We actually come from two very different backgrounds.

DEANA'S STORY

I didn't start doing this "frugal thing" until 1991. I had already been a stay-at-home mom with Katie for three years when Alex came along, and I felt a pressing need to pinch pennies.

My husband and I had been in our first home with its mortgage and responsibilities only two years when we added this new mouth to feed. Having an at-home parent was an unwavering commitment we made to our children. Living on just one income was not an extreme hardship, but it wasn't a cakewalk either. I credit my conversion to frugality to Amy Dacyczyn's book, *Tightwad Gazette*. I remember reading the pages ravenously, feeling as if I had stumbled on buried treasure.

My family's financial background didn't prepare me for a lifestyle of self-imposed downsizing. I came from a prosperous family from Oklahoma. My father earned a comfortable living in the oil industry. However, my parents did not come from families of means—quite the opposite. They diligently gave up months of lunch money in high school in order to buy their first car when they graduated and got married. They instilled in me that strong work ethic, but they also desired to give my sister and me "everything they never had." Consequently, I was never in want of anything, even luxuries. Please don't misunderstand! I'm not trying to brag nor am I ungrateful—my parents worked hard to give me these things. I'm just illustrating that no matter what your background, a simpler, more frugal lifestyle is possible and desirable. It can become your passion too.

Because of frugality, our family has been able to do one of our favorite things—give. Since choosing to live below our means, we have been able to give away 20 percent or more of our income every year. It is our greatest joy to give generously to worthy charities. Frugality allows us this freedom.

In 1993, our family moved to Texas, and I found my frugal friend, Angie. We bonded almost immediately and have been joined at the hip ever since. The Frugal Family Network is birthed not only from our great enthusiasm for thriftiness, but also our great sisterhood.

ANGIE'S STORY

I grew up on a farm in Nebraska as the last of five children. While I was making my first memorable trip to the store for "store-bought clothes," Deana was jetting off to New York for custom-made clothes. The store I visited wasn't Saks Fifth

Avenue. It was Skagway in Grand Island, Nebraska—a *few* blocks west of New York City.

My parents grew up in the depression, and they knew how to assess an item's value based on usefulness. I've thankfully inherited their wisdom and have been frugal my entire life. A boss once told me, "*You* could live like a queen on Social Security." But I've continued perfecting my skills of frugality. For example, I used to spend almost $400 a month to feed our family of four. I now spend around $135 while still providing a bountiful, nutritious table.

When I met Tom in 1988, he was making $18,000 a year. My salary was similar. We married in 1989. In 1991 when our first son, Timothy, was born, we both voiced our desire to build a home in the country. We had been "frugaling" for awhile, but now we had a mission for our thriftiness. We were able to buy the land with cash (we carry a mortgage on the house) and buy two vehicles with cash—all through black-belt frugality. In 1993 we moved into our home right before the birth of our second son, Adam. We are grateful for the power frugality has given us to live comfortably on one income.

Most likely your financial situation falls somewhere between ours. You may be a natural born frugalite, a thrift neophyte, or a tightwad wannabe. Wherever you are on the economic spectrum, we want you to draw from our past and current experiences to move toward a simpler and more frugal life.

We know folks that are struggling to make ends meet. We get emails from them every day. We know families that are struggling to live on one income so one parent can stay home with the children. We meet them at every workshop. So for all of you fighting the battle of the budget, we've filled this book with the best money-saving tips we could cram between the covers. Catch our passion for thrift, and financial freedom can be yours.

More Bags for Your Buck: Save on Groceries

Today when I (Deana) look at my grocery store receipts, I have a great sense of accomplishment. On average I spend $180 a month to feed a family of four. My frugal friend Angie does even better, spending only $135 a month.

It wasn't always this way. We used to spend $400 a month, and according to the Food Marketing Institute this isn't unusual. In fact, a family of four spends an average of $560 a month. Back then I thought the high cost was due to having an infant and a toddler at home; $40 cases of formula and $20 packages of disposable diapers would throw anybody's budget for a loop. But when my kids graduated from toddlerhood, I was still spending the same amount. I felt like I was spending more and more money, but had less and less food. I knew something had to change.

Angie and I pinpointed our problems and came up with solutions that cut our grocery bills by more than half. Want to see how we did it? Keep reading!

Serious Business

People spend a substantial amount on groceries each year, yet people fail to take it as seriously as they would a home or car loan. Writing a big check to the mortgage company gets our attention, but grocery costs accumulate over time, so people are often unaware of the total cost. Our advice is to approach grocery shopping with the attitude of a corporate procurement officer; it's your job to get the most from your food dollar. Get serious about grocery savings, and you'll save serious money.

Analyze Your Receipt

Look at your last grocery receipt and highlight the money wasters. Highlight convenience foods, highly processed products, and impulse items. Take note of any duplicates—products that do the same job as other items on the receipt. Mark specialty items that lack versatility and are used for only one recipe. Eliminate these things in favor of raw foods and basic, flexible ingredients. Highlighting these costly mistakes will help you avoid them in the future.

Make a List

Always make a list before you go shopping. Grocery lists will help you avoid guessing about what you need. Guessing often leads to buying items you already have. A list also helps you stay disciplined; if it's not on the list, don't buy it. I keep a recycled envelope on my refrigerator and jot down items as we need them. Inside the envelope I tuck in corresponding coupons.

My Momma Told Me, You Better Shop Around

Don't be loyal to one store; shop around. Compare prices between local supermarkets. Be willing to think of other options. You'll find bargains at farmer's markets, clearinghouses (like MacFrugals), discount stores, and warehouse stores. Shopping around is the best way to find the lowest prices.

Do Your Homework

The grocery industry is very competitive. Read stores' weekly ads to find the current best buys and "loss leaders"—items the grocery store is willing to take a "loss" on in order to "lead" you into their store.

Menu Planning

Arbitrarily planning a week's worth of menus is expensive. Instead, eat what's cheap. Use loss leaders and sale items to determine your menus. Your meals will follow the abundance of the seasons and be less expensive.

Shop Alone

I try to shop alone, leaving my spouse and children at home. Going alone allows me to concentrate solely on the task of getting the most for my money.

Don't Go to the Store When You're Hungry

This adage is simple but true. Also avoid going to the store when you're thirsty, tired, rushed, or grumpy. One summer Angie made the mistake of taking her two boys to the grocery store around lunchtime after an exhausting morning of swimming. They were starving! And as you might expect, they came home with much more food than they needed.

Don't Take a Cart

If your list is small, don't grab a cart out of habit. An empty cart is like a yawning chasm, begging to be filled. Take a hand-held basket instead. Or better yet, don't take anything at all because if you can't carry it, you can't buy it!

Get In, Get Out

The longer you stay, the more you pay. Industry experts say you'll spend an extra $2 for every minute you linger in the store after picking up what you need.

Store Layout

Stores are designed to make you pass as many items as possible. In order to get to the most frequently purchased items, you have to walk from one side of the store all the way to the other. Bread is usually at the opposite end of the store from the milk. The produce section typically has the highest profit margin, so it's often the first department you encounter upon entering the store. The wide "racetrack" around the perimeter of the store is designed to lead you past temptations in all the store's major departments. Be aware of this strategy. Take the most direct route to the items you need and avoid backtracking.

High and Low

Look for items on the upper and lower shelves; they're cheaper. Grocery stores put the most expensive products at eye level to tempt you into a convenient purchase. Some companies pay premium prices to the grocery store for this "real estate." Look low for more dough.

End Caps

Products stacked at the end of each aisle, known as "end caps," sometimes display sale items. But they're often paired with companion items that are not on sale. Be careful. They're also great selling locations for high-profit, impulse buys. Big displays don't always mean big savings.

Beware of Advertising

An average of forty-nine thousand products are available in a typical supermarket. Each package has roughly one seventeenth of a second to get your attention. With such a short time to be noticed, companies want to grab your attention before you even get to the store. So they bombard you with advertisements. They do their best to create consumer desire for their brand, but often the desire they create has nothing to do with the product. They say cereal will make you strong, shampoo will make you alluring, and frozen dinners will add hours to your day.

No product can live up to these promises, yet people are pulled in by the advertising, which is often highly emotional. Consumers buy groceries, half expecting them to satisfy their innermost yearnings; they're left with pesky wrappers and empty stomachs.

Distinguish between a want and a need. Choose products for their nourishment, not for their emotional appeal. You'll be better fed on less money.

Impulse Seat

If you do give in to a tempting store promotion, put that item in the child seat area of the cart and reconsider its value when you get to the checkout stand. Don't hesitate to give groceries to the checker, telling him or her that you've changed your mind. The items will be returned to the shelf, and you'll put more money in your wallet.

Coupons

Many people are surprised we don't automatically sing the praises of coupons. After all, we teach frugality; we ought to be coupons' biggest advocates, right? Well, not really. There is far more to reducing your grocery spending than clipping coupons.

Coupons were invented over a hundred years ago by an Atlanta druggist named Asa Candler. He gave away coupons to introduce people to a new product called Coca-Cola. Today coupons are used for the same reason. They introduce new products, increase sales, and foster brand loyalty. They aren't meant to be a gift to the consumer. They are a marketing tool. Also, coupons are most often issued for high-priced national products and convenience foods, so don't assume your coupons guarantee you the best deal.

Coupons can be helpful, however, if used wisely. Combine them with sales to get the best price. Ask the store if they will honor competitors' coupons. Combine manufacturer coupons with store coupons for extra savings. Look for stores that offer double coupons, but watch out, their overall prices are usually higher. Swap coupons with friends to get the best selection. Take advantage of rebate offers. Ask for a rain check if a discounted item is out of stock. And don't be tempted to buy a product just because you have a coupon.

We're halfway through our grocery trip; Angie will take it from here. She'll lead you up and down each aisle, so you can seize the deals and avoid the traps.

In our household my husband, Tom, is the breadwinner, but I (Angie) am the bread buyer. My job is equally important in helping our financial ship stay afloat.

Bagged Is Better

Buy prebagged produce rather than individual produce items. This one tip will save you a *lot* of money. Individual potatoes cost about $.89 a pound. A 20-pound bag of potatoes on sale costs $1.98. So, if you buy the bag, you spend $.10 a pound and get nine times more food than if you buy individual potatoes. Also, while the weight printed on the bag is the minimum weight required, we've found they're often heavier!

Sound like a lot of produce? Freeze what you can't use right away. I (Angie) buy 3-pound bags of onions. When I get home I chop them in my food processor and freeze them. When a recipe calls for onion, I pull out the frozen onions and break off what I need. Also, you can use ice cube trays to freeze any foods that are mushy and runny (like homemade baby food). When the cubes have hardened, pop them out and store them in a freezer bag. One cube equals about one tablespoon.

Use It All

Buy 100 percent consumable produce when possible. Examples are zucchinis and potatoes because you can eat their skins, which contain nutritious fiber. However, the majority of a watermelon goes to the compost pile. The difference between all-consumed and partially consumed food can be significant to your wallet.

Worth the Weight

If paying by pound, shake excess water from leafy vegetables and pinch off empty branches from a bunch of grapes. Why pay for something you aren't going to eat?

Buy What's in Season

Buying fruits and vegetables in season is a good idea. They will be at their peak flavor for the best price.

Build Relationships

Get acquainted with the department managers. They will be more likely to give discounts to someone they know. I routinely ask the produce manager if he will mark down the lone bananas sitting forlornly next to the plump, intact bunches. Also, ask for a sample. Most stores will "plug" a watermelon to be sure it's a good one. (Remember, watermelons are only partially consumable, so when you do buy one, make sure it's tasty!)

Pretty Produce

Good looks reign in the produce department, so the bins are culled daily to assure only the best are displayed. While culled fruits and veggies won't sell next to their more attractive peers, often they're still perfectly acceptable. Ask the produce manager if you may have these snubbed fruits and veggies for free. The place where our store puts these is called "the produce box."

Reduced for Quick Sale

Meat is often associated with costly meals. But it doesn't have to be expensive. We enjoy a variety of meats without the pricey markup by nabbing meats marked "Reduced for Quick Sale." These are meats near their expiration date, so the store drastically lowers the price per pound. A product at its expiration date does not mean it's unsafe. It only reflects guidelines for optimum quality issued by the meat industry. We use this meat the same day or freeze it for later. Normally I get meat for a third of its original price.

Wheeling and Dealing

Department managers have more authority over price reductions than you may realize. If you see a package that is about to expire but is not marked down, ask the butcher for a discount. One evening I saw fully cooked roast beef marked "Reduced for Quick Sale." The roasts were regularly $6.59 a pound, but had been reduced to $1.50 a pound. There were almost twenty roasts on sale and it was 7 P.M. I told the meat department manager I would buy all the roasts if he reduced them to a dollar a pound. He looked at his watch and told me I had myself a deal.

Many Thanksgiving turkeys and Easter hams won't be sold, and they will all have similar expiration dates. Note that date on your calendar and ask the butcher what time of day they mark down the meats. A well-timed trip to the store may net you significant savings.

Don't Pay for Processing

Processing equals cost. With a sharp knife and a will to save money, you can do some processing. Instead of buying pieces of chicken, buy a whole roasting chicken and cut it at home. Many butchers will provide a little extra processing at the meat counter for free, such as tenderizing or slicing a ham for lunchmeat.

Deli Department

Entering the deli department can make you weak in the wallet. Suddenly good dollar sense is replaced by the savory aroma of roasting chicken. Our advice is to go right past this department before the free samples suck you in. But if you happen to get detained, here are some important things to keep in mind.

According to my brother-in-law, Joe Zalewski, the former manager of a Dominick's deli in Chicago, the best buys are the unadvertised in-store specials. "When extra meats are shipped in, there is an impromptu sale to clear space," Joe told me. "Ask the deli associate if there are any great deals of the day." Joe also advises having lunchmeat sliced thin; it will go further when making a sandwich at home. Moreover, the deli may include the ends of cheese or lunchmeat free with your purchase, if you ask.

Many freshly made items are reduced in the evening or the next morning. A hot roasted chicken that was full price one day will be wrapped and sold cold for half price the next day.

Bakery

Bypass the supermarket bakery and shop at a bakery that sells day-old breads or a bread thrift store. I buy high-fiber bread for $.39 at the bread store. Compared to $1.69 at the supermarket, the extra trip is worth the savings per loaf. Bread freezes well, so stock up when you're there.

Most things in the bakery can be made at home with a little practice. I make homemade Italian bread for about $.19 a loaf. Compared to the $1.99 store price, homemade bread always wins.

Cheaper Cheese

The best price on cheese is found in larger blocks. If you want a single slice of cheese, just grab a knife. Shredding it yourself with a food processor can save you up to a dollar per pound. Cheese freezes well, so don't be afraid to stock up when you see a terrific sale. Another way to buy cheese at a good price is at the self-service salad bar in your grocery store. Most salad bars charge per pound. If the cost per pound is better at the salad bar than in the dairy case, do your cheese shopping at the salad bar.

Everyday Eggs

At about 8¢ each, eggs are very economical. Around Easter stores have super deals on eggs. Capitalize on these deals by using them in a quiche and freezing it. In addition to saving you money, this will supply you with a quick meal from the freezer.

If you have an allergy to eggs or want to save even more money, in baking recipes substitute each egg with one heaping tablespoon of soy flour plus two tablespoons of water. This soy flour substitute costs less than a penny.

Cost-Per-Unit Calculation

How do you know which ketchup size is really the best value? You don't, unless you figure the cost per unit. To do this, take the price and divide it by the number of "units" (e.g., ounces).

Example: $1.98 ÷ 64 oz. = 3¢ per oz.

When you know this info, it will be easy to select the best value for your money. Some stores have the cost per unit listed on the shelf tag. However, products tossed in a clearance bin will not. I keep a small calculator in my purse to do a quick calculation when necessary.

Price Keeper

Have you ever come out of a warehouse store wondering if you got a good deal? You can know for sure with a "Price Keeper." To make one, you'll need a notebook. Write a letter of the alphabet on each page. These letters correspond to foods purchased (e.g., cheese goes under *C*). Using recent receipts identify twenty products that you purchase often. For each item write a store code (e.g., *W* = Walmart), item and brand, and then the price and size. Finally, calculate the cost per unit. Record only the best price you've found. The next time you're in a warehouse store, you can refer to your Price Keeper to find out whether their ketchup six-pack is a better deal than the grocery store's ketchup. Use your Price Keeper at other stores too.

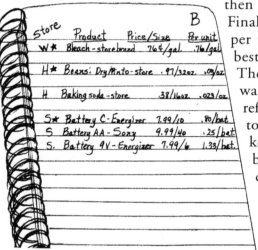

My price comparisons have yielded surprising results. The discount stores have the best price for over-the-counter medicines and toiletries, selling shaving cream for almost a dollar less than at the grocery store! The bread store beat every place for bakery items. The warehouse store is the best place for cheese, but not for many other items. And I was able to confirm which grocery store had the lowest prices. The Price Keeper was the final step that brought my grocery bill down to an average of $135 a month.

Bulk Purchase Principle

When you hit a great clearance sale or super loss leader, stock up. Watch for expiration dates and buy only enough to last to the next sale. When a fancy grocery store opened in our area, they ran a special on Minute Maid apple juice for $.49 a can.

It's normally $1.49 a can. I went to the store, picked up two cases of juice, and went right to the checkout stand; I avoided the other, overpriced items in the store. By bulk purchasing I saved a dollar per can. That's a savings of $48.

Store Brands

Products with store brands are actually national-brand products with a different label. Your local grocery store sends out a contract for a particular product and asks for bids on the contract. National companies bid on the contract, and your store selects a supplier. This explains why store-brand products are often as good as anything else on the market, not to mention a whole lot cheaper. Don't be shy of those store brands!

Pounds of Price

If you remember only one thing from this chapter, remember this: skip the highly processed snack foods. They are expensive and nutritionally void. Many snacks in the chip aisle cost over $6 a pound! Most people wouldn't pay that for a choice cut of meat but pitch chips in the cart every time. Save money and choose healthier alternatives.

Check Out

Once you're in "the chute," otherwise known as a checkout lane, you're surrounded by items that have the highest markup in the store. Be careful. These impulse items can have a profit margin of 400 percent.

As the clerk scans the products, watch to ensure accuracy. Some stores have a scan guarantee that gives you the product free if it scans wrong. But it's up to you to catch it. Find out what your store's policy is.

❧

"Nothing makes food less fattening than too high a price."

Cooking Up a Plate of Savings

Deana admits that before her frugal conversion, she wasn't the greatest cook. She often joked that her family's favorite thing for dinner was reservations. So we agreed that I (Angie) would write the chapter on cooking.

I lowered my grocery bill by focusing on three things: (1) "power" grocery shopping, as detailed in chapter 1, (2) reducing waste, and (3) smart cooking techniques. If I'm power grocery shopping to get the best price on our food but preparing it expensively or wastefully, I haven't gained anything. This chapter includes tricks to reduce your waste, frugal cooking tips, and frugal recipes.

Freezer Stock

Freezer stock is what you get when you save vegetable broth and other flavored liquids. When I steam veggies, I pour the broth from the pan into a plastic container. The water has great flavor and many nutrients that are usually poured down the drain. I pop the container in my freezer and add to it. When steak sauce or ketchup bottles are empty, I put water in the bottle, swish it around, and add the liquid to the freezer stock container. If you've never done this before, it might sound odd, but give it a try. You'll be surprised at how good it tastes. Freezer stock is perfect for any recipe that calls for broth. I cook rice in it because it reduces stickiness and makes an otherwise bland side dish flavorful.

This can be done with solid food too. When only a tablespoon of corn or a few bits of meat are left at the end of a meal, I put them in a plastic bag and store the bag in the freezer. When the freezer stock container is full, I add the bag of veggies and meat and we have soup! It's a free meal from something that may have been discarded.

Evaporated Milk Substitute
Mix powdered milk at half the dilution recommended on the box. This costs a fraction of canned evaporated milk.

Jalapeño Potato Soup
Here's a great way to use freezer stock and evaporated milk substitute.

1	medium onion chopped
¼	cup margarine
5	pounds of potatoes
8	cups chicken or veggie broth ("freezer stock")
1	teaspoon cumin or comino
½	cup chopped jalapeños (add as much "heat" as you like)
	Pinch of baking soda
4	cups evaporated milk (frugal substitute)
	Salt and pepper to taste

Optional Garnishes:
sour cream, bell pepper, chives, or paprika

In a large pot sauté onion in margarine until softened. Add potatoes, broth, and cumin. Cover and cook until potatoes are tender, about 30 minutes. When done, add jalapeños, baking soda, and evaporated milk. Mash potatoes with potato masher in the pot. Add salt and pepper to taste. Simmer about 20 minutes. Garnish each bowl with a dollop of sour cream, a ring of bell pepper, chives, or a sprinkle of paprika for color.

My cost to prepare this large batch of soup is only $1.38. This recipe will serve three large dinners and several lunches.

Turkey Broth

After you've taken the last bit of meat from a turkey, take the carcass, put it in a large pot with 6 cups of water and simmer. The water will turn to broth, which can be used in other recipes.

Frugalizing a Recipe

Learning to "frugalize" a recipe with costly ingredients is key to economical cooking. Some ingredients may be worth the price, but most can be substituted with a cheaper and healthier item.

Below is a list of ingredients for a standard recipe and next to it is my frugalized version. This will give you an idea of how to frugalize any recipe.

Breakfast Casserole (Original Recipe)

  5 eggs (8¢ x 5 = 40¢)
 12 ounces frozen hash browns ($2.29)
  1 cup shredded Provolone cheese ($1.65)
  1 large scallion chopped (20¢)
  ½ cup ricotta cheese (33¢)
  1 teaspoon salt (nominal cost)
  1 teaspoon pepper (nominal cost)
      Dash of hot sauce (nominal cost)
      Paprika (nominal cost)
  6 slices cooked Canadian bacon ($1.25)
Total $6.12

Breakfast Casserole (Frugalized)

  5 eggs (8¢ x 5 = 40¢)
 12 ounces shredded potatoes (3¢)
  1 cup shredded cheddar cheese (79¢)
  ½ cup regular onion chopped (from freezer)
  ½ cup homemade yogurt (9¢)
  1 teaspoon salt (nominal cost)
  1 teaspoon pepper (nominal cost)
      Serve salsa on the side (nominal cost)
      Paprika (nominal cost)
      Meat ($0—see below)
Total $1.31 (That's almost a $5 savings for just one recipe!)

Here are the money-saving substitutions I made:

- I saved $2.26 by shredding fresh potatoes in the food processor rather than buying prepackaged frozen hash browns! A 20-pound bag of spuds on a great sale is 98¢ (5¢ per pound). A typical sale is $1.98 (10¢ per pound). By not using the packaged hash browns, I saved money and eliminated the chemicals and preservatives that go with them.

- By using homemade yogurt and less expensive cheese I saved another dollar.

- I used leftover ham, but if you wanted, you could skip the meat. If you add meat, sprinkle it on top rather than mixing it in. You'll use less of this costly ingredient but still enjoy the flavor.

To cook the above recipe, add all ingredients, sprinkle top with paprika, and bake at 350°F for 45 minutes to an hour. Next time you come across a great recipe, frugalize it to save money and increase nutrition!

Expiration Freezology

If an item is about to expire, either use it or freeze it. These foods can be thawed later and used in casseroles or baking. Once when I got back from a vacation, I discovered I had forgotten a gallon of milk in our refrigerator; it had soured. Rather than throw the milk away, I froze it in two cup portions, and then used it for baking cakes.

Freeze extra garden produce as well, such as tomatoes. To freeze tomatoes, boil whole tomatoes for about a minute. Remove them from the water and let them cool. The skins slip right off. Freeze in quart-sized bags.

Texas Tornado Salsa

To use up your extra garden tomatoes, make this delicious homemade salsa, which freezes nicely.

½   medium onion, chopped
6   jalapeño peppers (seeds removed)
2   garlic cloves, crushed

10 medium garden tomatoes (seeds removed)
3   tablespoons lemon juice
½   bunch cilantro (I use the leaves only)
1   teaspoon cumin
    pinch of salt
1   can of crushed tomatoes (optional)

In food processor blend together onions, peppers, and garlic. Add tomatoes. Blend in lemon juice, salt, cumin, and cilantro. If you want thicker salsa, add crushed tomatoes.

Better Beans

A friend sent us this blooper from a church bulletin: "Bean supper Tuesday night at 6 P.M. Music will follow." Though beans have gotten a bad rap for their "musical" aftereffects, they are exceptionally nutritious and one of the most frugal foods. "When served with grains like rice or corn bread," reports Purely American health food company, "beans are a complete protein in the same quantity and quality as meat."

Store-brand dry beans are your best buy at around 45¢ a pound. Two cups dry beans (1 pound) equals 6 cups cooked beans, which is only 5¢ a serving! It's hard to beat that price for such a nutritional food. To prepare dry beans:

- *Rinse and soak.* Rinse the beans thoroughly and set them in a bowl. Fill the bowl with water until there is 3 inches of water above the beans. Changing out the water a couple times during soaking will reduce the amount of complex sugars, which are what give people that "musical" aftereffect. For convenience you can let them soak overnight.

- *Cook.* Using 3 cups of water for every 1 cup of soaked beans, pour beans and water into a pot. Simmer until beans are tender, about 45 minutes to an hour. Do not add salt or any acidic ingredients until beans are tender or you'll end up with hard beans.

Pineapple Beans

    2   cups dry beans
    1   pound ground beef, ground turkey, or sausage
    1   chopped clove garlic
    1   large onion
    1   can (20 ounces) crushed pineapple
    1   cup barbecue sauce
    2   tablespoons soy sauce
    1   teaspoon salt
    1   teaspoon pepper

Cook beans until tender. Brown ground beef with onion and garlic, drain. Add ground beef to cooked beans. Add remaining ingredients and simmer for 30 minutes. Serve over rice or with corn bread.

Bean Recycling

If your beans come out too firm, send them through your food processor and use them for bean burritos. Or, add salsa and make a spicy bean dip.

Frugal Minute Rice

Pick up a bag of regular white rice, which is about ⅓ the cost of brand name Minute Rice. Into a pot pour one part rice to two parts water or freezer stock. Cover and bring to a boil for one minute. Turn off the heat and leave covered. The rice will finish cooking on its own. This is a frugal version of brand name Minute Rice.

Meal Stretchers

To make your main dish go further, avoid serving meat as an entrée by itself. Instead, combine it with a meal stretcher like pasta, beans, rice, or potatoes. This may sound like plain fare but just think, these meal stretchers are part of chicken divan, beef stroganoff, and good ol' chili.

Creative Casseroles

The all-purpose casserole is a winner for using up leftovers. A casserole combines four things: (1) meat, (2) vegetables, (3) a meal stretcher, and (4) sauce or "binder." Use any cooked meat, add leftover vegetables and a meal stretcher. And the key to a tasty casserole is the binder. Most Americans use canned cream soup as the binder. But at almost a dollar a can, there is a much better and healthier option. Below is a cream soup recipe that you can make from scratch. It's as old as the hills and for good reason; it costs only 17¢ per serving!

Cream Soup Master Mix

This recipe is for a dry mix to which you can add water for a great cream soup substitute. You can store it in a canister like you do with flour and sugar. It makes several cups of cream soup.

2½ cups flour (or 1½ cups cornstarch)
2 cups dry milk
½ cup bouillon powder
2 tablespoons onion powder
1 teaspoon basil
1 teaspoon oregano
1 teaspoon pepper

Combine all ingredients in a plastic container. When making a casserole, combine ½ cup flour mix (or ⅓ cup cornstarch mix) with 1½ cups water; this makes the equivalent of one can of cream soup. Combine with the other casserole ingredients.

Chicken and Rice Casserole

1 small onion, chopped
3 celery stalks, chopped
¼ cup margarine
3 cups broth or freezer stock
1 cup uncooked rice
4 cups cooked chicken or turkey
1 can cream soup (or frugal substitute)
½ cup shredded cheese
1 teaspoon liquid smoke

Preheat oven to 350°F. Sauté onion and celery in melted margarine until tender. Add broth and rice. Cook until rice is tender. Stir in remaining ingredients and pour into casserole dish. Bake uncovered 20 minutes.

Fruitful Marinade

Make a great marinade by saving the juice from canned pineapple and adding it to soy sauce. Add other seasonings as desired.

Crock-Pot Cooking

Many homes have a forgotten Crock-Pot under their counter . . . somewhere. Dust it off and put it to use! A Crock-Pot can be a frugal lifesaver. By knowing your dinner will be ready when you get home, you won't be tempted to buy drive-thru food at suppertime. Here's a good recipe to put your Crock-Pot to use.

Zingy Hawaiian Chicken

1   roasting chicken
1   cup teriyaki sauce
1   can pineapple (chunks or crushed)
1   can stewed tomatoes with green chilies (or fresh garden tomatoes and jalapeños)

Place all ingredients in a Crock-Pot and cook 6–8 hours on low.

Milk Money

Powdered milk costs about a third less than bottled milk. Mix it half and half with a jug of milk for drinking. Or keep a small amount in your refrigerator and use in baking when the recipe calls for milk.

That's a Wrap

Save stick margarine wrappers and use them to grease your pans when baking.

Piece of Cake

One of the easiest ways to save money on a party is to make the cake yourself. It's easy to do. Just keep it simple. A sheet cake with frosting and sprinkles will cover the bill. Or spell out Happy Birthday with store-brand M&Ms.

Mom's Chocolate Sheet Cake

Here is my mom's sheet cake recipe. It goes all the way back to World War II, so it has stood the test of time! I use it any time I need a party cake.

2	cups white sugar
2	cups flour
½	cup margarine
½	cup oil
3½	tablespoons cocoa
1	cup water
½	cup soured milk
2	eggs
1	teaspoon baking soda
1	teaspoon vanilla

Preheat oven to 400°F. Mix sugar and flour in a bowl. Bring margarine, oil, cocoa, and water to a boil, and then pour the mixture over sugar and flour. Beat together milk, eggs, baking soda, and vanilla. Mix in with other ingredients. Bake in a greased and floured 15" x 12" x 1" pan for 20 to 25 minutes.

Chocolate Sheet Cake Frosting

½	cup margarine
3½	tablespoons cocoa
6	tablespoons milk
1	pound powdered sugar
1	teaspoon vanilla

Mix and heat margarine, cocoa, and milk. Remove from heat and add sugar and vanilla. Whip until smooth. Spread on cool cake.

Powdered Elegance

To decorate your cake quickly at minimal cost, place a doily on your cake and lightly dust it with powdered sugar. Lift the doily to leave an elegant design.

Coffee in Dessert

If you love cappuccino-flavored desserts and breads, refrigerate leftover coffee and use it as the liquid ingredient in desserts, breads, and muffin recipes.

Food Processor Kneading

For a long time I avoided making breads because of the kneading involved. I have a busy-bee nature, so standing in one spot, kneading dough for 10 minutes, is not my idea of a good time. Then I discovered my food processor could do the work in a fraction of the time and still produce wonderful dough. I place the dough into my food processor and spin it around about 20 rotations. The dough should "clean" the sides of the food processor. If the mixture is too wet, add a sprinkle of flour. If it's too dry or stiff, add a couple drops of water. This will save your wrists, your time, and your sanity! Here is a recipe you can use to practice food processor kneading.

Mom's Cinnamon Rolls

1	cup milk
½	cup margarine
½	cup sugar
1	teaspoon salt
2	tablespoons yeast
3½	to 5 cups flour
1	egg

Filling:

	cinnamon
1	cup brown sugar
½	cup margarine
	raisins (if desired)

1. Heat milk to 120°F (1 minute and 20 seconds in my microwave). Add margarine. In a large bowl combine sugar, salt, yeast, and 1 cup flour. Add heated milk and margarine. Mix 1 minute. Beat in egg and 1 cup flour. Mix 2 more minutes.

2. Stir in 1½ cups flour with a wooden spoon. Knead dough on floured surface about 10 minutes or in food processor. Put in greased bowl, cover with dishcloth, and let rise in warm place for 1 hour. Dough should double in size.

3. Punch down dough, put on floured surface, cover with bowl, and let rest 15 minutes.

4. Roll dough into an 18″ x 10″ rectangle. Sprinkle with cinnamon, brown sugar, and melted margarine. Roll up jelly-roll style, pinch seam shut, and cut 1-inch slices. Place in greased and floured pan. Cover and let rise about 45 minutes.

5. Bake at 375° for 20–25 minutes. When cooled, glaze with icing (1 cup powdered sugar and 2 tablespoons milk).

You're on a Roll

Imagine your family waking up to the smell of hot fresh cinnamon rolls. This is possible without your having to get up at 4 A.M. Mix up a batch of rolls the night before and let them rise in the pan. Then cover the pan with plastic wrap and refrigerate overnight. In the morning set out the rolls and let them rise completely while the oven is heating, then bake. You can freeze an uncooked pan of rolls. It's great to have a couple of pans in the freezer for unexpected company.

Pancake Syrup

Pancake syrup can be made from scratch for about half the price of store-brand syrup. Mix 1 cup sugar, ½ cup water, 2 tablespoons molasses or corn syrup, 1 teaspoon maple flavoring, and 1 teaspoon butter flavoring. Stir over low heat until the sugar is completely dissolved. Bring to a boil. Boil for 3 minutes without stirring. To make a fancy syrup, mix one cup of pancake syrup with 3 tablespoons of orange juice and 1 teaspoon margarine. Serve warm.

A Better Breakfast

Last year my son's elementary school class went on a field trip to Sea World in San Antonio. The bus left at 6:30 A.M., but lunch wasn't until noon. Knowing there would be a long time between meals, Timothy ate a leftover hamburger for breakfast. This may sound strange, but during the field trip most of the kids were "starving" and cranky by 9 A.M. Timothy was happy and energetic, and he made it to lunchtime without a problem. His breakfast was less expensive than cold cereal, which costs as much as $6 a pound, and because of the protein content it sustained him better.

So now you're saying, "OK, frugal ladies. If I don't feed my kids cereal, what are they going to eat?" Good question. There are many nutritionally sound alternatives to a bowl of cold cereal. Here are several:

- muffins (6¢ each, see recipe on pages 32–33)
- pancakes or waffles (5¢ each)
- hot oatmeal (3¢ per serving)
- baked potato (5¢ each)
- corn bread (3¢ each)
- any meal leftovers (price varies)
- pigs in a blanket (13¢ each, see recipe on page 25)
- breakfast tacos (9¢ each, see recipe below)

I make all of the above from scratch, but I don't cook every morning. I make a triple batch of pancakes, for example, serve some and freeze the rest. Or I cook a lot of breakfast sausage, freeze it, and assemble it into breakfast tacos in the morning.

Nontraditional foods are excellent too. A hot baked potato is very satisfying, especially if it's sprinkled with cheese and crumbled sausage. I have the boys drink or eat protein in the morning (milk, yogurt, cheese, or meat). This will stay with them longer than a carbohydrate alone.

Breakfast Tacos

On a tortilla, spoon cooked crumbled sausage, scrambled eggs, potatoes (leftover hash browns or baked potatoes), cheese, and salsa. All of these items can be precooked and stored in the freezer. It takes less than a minute to heat up a breakfast taco in the microwave.

Pigs in a Blanket

There are two ways to make pigs in a blanket. The first is made with pancakes. Cook link sausage and pancakes and wrap each link in a pancake. Secure with toothpick and serve with fruit or syrup. The second way to make pigs in a blanket is with dough. Cook the sausage links and wrap them in uncooked bread or biscuit dough. Place them on a baking sheet and bake according to your bread or biscuit recipe, usually 400°F for 12 minutes. These also freeze well. Just pop them in a freezer bag and reheat for a quick breakfast.

❧

"We were so poor, we got married just for the rice!"
—Unknown

Money-Saving Munchies: Lunches and Snacks for Less

Do you want to put $25 in your pocket right now? Pack your lunch! Once during our weekly appearance on the local CBS TV station (KEYE-42), we did a lunch box cost comparison. Lunch box #1 contained a Lunchable. Most parents already know this is an expensive option. The one we used cost $3.05. That's more than a hot lunch at school.

Parents instinctively know they can pack a lunch for less, which brings us to lunch box #2. If the lunch box is full of over-processed, overpackaged snacks, it could cost more than you realize. Lunch box #2 contained turkey sticks, a yogurt cup with sprinkles, pretzel Goldfish, Moo Town cheese sticks, a Rice Krispy bar, and a juice box. The final cost came to a whopping $3.20!

Now for the grand finale—the healthier and cheaper frugal lunch box #3. For this lunch box we packed the same items as were in lunch box #2, but gave them a frugal makeover. We packed a spider sandwich (7¢) (see below), homemade yogurt (9¢) with sprinkles (2¢), a bag of pretzels (3¢), cheese sticks cut from a block of cheese (7¢), a homemade rice cereal bar made with store-brand ingredients (4¢), and a water bottle (0¢) instead of the overpriced juice box. Our lunch came out to 32¢! That's one-tenth the price of lunch box #2 but with similar foods.

You can do this too. It just takes some frugal creativity and a commitment to making a healthier, less expensive lunch alternative. Here are our ideas for making lunches and snacks cheaper and even healthier for your family.

Spider Sandwich

A little creativity makes a frugal lunch the highlight of the day! Surprise your kids with a spider sandwich in their lunch box. This trick uses ordinary, inexpensive food and jazzes it up. Using two pieces of bread and a cup, stamp out 2 circles of bread. Spread peanut butter between the slices. Add 8 pretzel sticks for legs and 2 raisins or chocolate chips for eyes. To add to the arachnid theme, draw a spider's web on a white disposable napkin.

When my (Angie's) son, Timothy, took this sandwich to school, it was all the rave at his lunch table. Apparently the news traveled quickly because another child's mother contacted me for the recipe. At the class's request I made 18 spider sandwiches with accompanying web napkins and brought them for a class snack.

Sandwich Sensation

The spider sandwich success launched me into a brief phase of sandwich creativity. I experimented with various foods to see how many different animal sandwiches I could create. My boys' favorites were a porcupine sandwich (circle sandwich with several pretzels sticking straight up from the top), a mouse sandwich (teardrop-shaped sandwich with pretzel whiskers and a curved pretzel tail), and a pig sandwich (circle sandwich with ⅓ marshmallow slice for a snout, raisins for eyes, and pretzel sticks inserted to form triangles for ears). I send these sandwiches in plastic containers rather than sandwich bags to preserve their shape. These sandwiches make frugality fun!

Super Spatula

Use a spatula to scrape out peanut butter, mustard, jelly, or mayonnaise jars. The extra effort will rescue ingredients for another sandwich, or more!

Roll Up the Savings

The versatile tortilla is perfect for your child's lunch box, and it's cheap too! Layer a tortilla with meat, cheese, or veggies. Then roll it up. Slice it on an angle into three pieces. Wrap tightly in foil or plastic.

You can also make a quick quesadilla for a snack. Lay a tortilla on a plate, sprinkle it with cheese, then lay another tortilla on top. Either melt it in the oven on low or heat in the microwave. Slice the quesadilla into wedges with a pizza cutter.

Wonderful Water

Pack a water bottle for lunch rather than juice or milk. Fill a sport bottle halfway with water and freeze. In the morning fill the rest of the bottle with water. The water bottle will act as an ice pack and a drink. At the end of the day when you are emptying the drink container, you won't be pouring out juice or milk, which essentially is money down the drain. You will be pouring out leftover water, which costs next to nothing.

Encore Meals

Don't let good food go bad. Designate one shelf in your refrigerator for leftovers and use them first.

You Crack Me Up

To revive soggy or stale crackers, place them on a cookie sheet and bake at 350°F until crisp.

Peanut Butter Crackers

Spread peanut butter or cream cheese between two crackers. These homemade cracker snacks are cheaper than the store-bought kind and they taste better too.

Homemade Lunchable

Make a homemade Lunchable by cutting out circles of cheese and lunchmeat with a clean pill bottle. Add crackers and serve in a plastic container that has multiple compartments. Deana and I each had a coupon for a free Lunchable. After the kids ate the contents, we kept the plastic container and filled it with our own items. We covered the tray with plastic wrap and secured it with a rubber band.

Hidden Heels

To use up bread heels, spread peanut butter on the outside of the heel, then flip it over so it becomes the inside of the sandwich. That way you still have a soft side of bread on the outside, which will help the sandwich pass the inspection of picky eaters.

A Wave of Savings

I recently saw prepackaged wavy cheese sticks in the dairy case for 53¢ an ounce. That's $8.50 a pound! They were called "wave runners," cleverly packaged with a surfing theme. After smirking at the over-the-top marketing of this simple product, I came home and made the same thing. Armed with my handy dandy crinkle cutter and cheese that cost $1.59 a pound at a warehouse store, I sliced several "Zalewski Wave Runners" for the boys' snack. We all rode the wave of savings on that one!

Mommy Marketing

If your kids are picky eaters, employ some mommy marketing techniques. For example, when bananas start getting brown spots on them, let your kids know that anyone can eat a plain ol' monkey banana, but this is an exotic giraffe banana! Have the kids pretend they are giants who are going to munch down the "trees" (aka broccoli). See if they can eat all the ants off the branch before the ants jump; ants are raisins on a branch of celery filled with peanut butter.

Pizza Power

Leftover pizza is a super treat in a lunch box. Though it's a favorite, it can be pricey if you buy it from a restaurant. Deana learned this the hard way. Her family adopted the habit of ordering two pizzas delivered from a national chain every Friday. By spending $17 every week, it added up to over $60 a month; that's $720 a year! Deana vowed to use that money for more important things and dived into doing the pizza herself. Making your own dough and using your own toppings and sauce is the cheapest, tastiest, and most nutritious way to go. Obviously, even a homemade pizza can be expensive if you load it with costly ingredients, so use leftovers like hamburger meat, veggies, and spaghetti sauce. Go easy on the cheese. Here is a great recipe for pizza dough.

Homemade Pizza Dough
1   cup warm water (105°–115°F)
1   tablespoon yeast (purchase yeast in bulk for the best price)
1   teaspoon sugar
2–3 cups flour
1   tablespoon vegetable oil
¾   teaspoon salt

Pour ¾ cup warm water into small bowl. Add sugar and yeast. Stir until yeast dissolves. Let stand 5 minutes, until foamy. In a food processor combine flour, oil, and salt. Pulse to combine, about 5 seconds. Add the yeast mixture and process 10 seconds. Drizzle in remaining water until a dough ball forms, then whirl for 20 rotations. Add more flour (if needed) until the dough is smooth, not tacky. Smooth the dough out with fingers on a floured surface. Oil a pan and lightly dust the surface with cornmeal or bread crumbs. Put dough on pan. Top with desired toppings. Bake at 425°F for 15–20 minutes. Yields one thick crust or two thin crusts.

Fruit Leather

Fruit leather or Fruit Roll-Ups is my kids' favorite snack. By making it at home I avoid the sugars and artificial ingredients found in store-bought products. Plus, I save a lot of money. To make fruit leather, use one piece of aluminum foil to form a boat approximately 9″ x 6″ with sides 1″ high. Place the foil boat on a shallow cookie sheet. Pour two cups of apple or pear sauce into the foil. Bake at 350°F for 30 minutes, then turn the oven down to 150° and cook for 8–10 hours. Peel the fruit leather off of the aluminum foil and store it in the refrigerator. For more pizzazz add food coloring and a small amount of flavoring, like strawberry, before baking. Stamp out shapes with cookie cutters for more fun. Here is a recipe for apple or pear sauce.

Homemade Apple or Pear Sauce

5–10 apples or pears
¼–½ cup water
1 teaspoon cinnamon

Peel, core, and slice fruit. Place the slices in a 3-quart saucepan with water and cover. Simmer until fruit is tender and begins to appear translucent. Add spice. Remove from heat and zip through your food processor. Store in the refrigerator. You can also mix in fruits like strawberries or peaches prior to cooking.

Banana on a Stick

Want a great way to get your kids to eat more fruit? Make a banana popsicle. Peel a banana, dip it in chocolate sauce, insert a Popsicle stick, and roll it in crushed nuts and freeze. Another version of this is to cut bananas into chunks, dip them in chocolate sauce, and then freeze. They resemble bon bons when you serve them. And, boy, will the kids gobble up this fruit snack!

Smoothies

Smoothies are an excellent way to use overripe, but still edible, fruit. Even my seven-year-old son, Adam, who prides himself that no fruit shall ever pass his lips, drinks smoothies. The trick to making smoothies that look and taste like ice cream is using frozen fruit. Take equal parts of frozen fruits (bananas and strawberries are a great combination) and chop them slightly in your food processor. Add apple juice until the liquid comes to the top of the fruit and blend until creamy smooth. Adding homemade yogurt or protein powder is a great way to provide even more nutrition to this fabulous treat.

Fruit Muffins Mix

Muffins are a tasty snack, a perfect lunch box addition. At 6¢ to 7¢ each they're economical too. That's a bargain, no matter how you slice it. The following recipe uses bananas, but it's versatile; you can substitute just about any fruit puree like applesauce or pear sauce.

1	cup margarine
4	cups sugar
4	eggs
1	teaspoon salt
1	teaspoon baking soda
½	cup buttermilk
4	cups flour
1	tablespoon vanilla
2	cups mashed bananas
	Pecans, walnuts, or chocolate chips (optional)

Cream margarine and sugar. Add eggs and vanilla. Add salt and baking soda to buttermilk. (If you don't have buttermilk, you can sour regular milk by adding ½ teaspoon vinegar.) Alternate mixing flour and buttermilk into creamed ingredients. Mix bananas until creamy and add to mixture. Pour into greased and floured bread pans, muffin cups, or cake pan. Add nuts, chocolate chips, or coconut to the top. Bake for 30 minutes at 350°F for cupcakes, 35 minutes for cakes, and 1 hour for bread loaves. Test with toothpick or knife for doneness. Let cool slightly before removing from pans. This makes a large batch of muffins or 3 loaves of bread.

Pack and Save

Start saving for that vacation, retirement, or newer car now. If you take your lunch to work, just twice a week, you will save over $500 a year. Skipping your daily designer coffee will yield almost $800 in a year's time. Then you can direct this money toward more important family goals.

"There are clues that tell you how much a restaurant will cost. If the word "cuisine" appears, it will be expensive. If the word "food" is used, it's moderately priced. If the sign says "eats," the food will be cheap but your medical bills will be quite high."
—*George Carlin*

Wait! Don't Throw That Away: Creative Recycling

I (Angie) used to love watching *MacGyver*, the TV show about a resourceful crime fighter who could get out of any dire situation. In almost every episode he would engineer a rescue using whatever was available. He would dig in his pockets and produce a paper clip, a stick of gum, and a calculator. With these he would create a radio to call in an air strike on the bad guys. Just think what MacGyver could have done if he had been a mom! With the contents of a purse and a diaper bag he probably could have created a small nuclear device. I doubt MacGyver threw away much. He knew it was often possible to make something useful out of things that were headed for the trash.

We've never had to fight international terrorists, but Deana and I know the value of making do with what we have. Instead of looking for a retail solution to all our needs, we recycle! Here are some things we've made out of everyday trash.

Dishwasher Caddy

If you wash small items like pacifiers, sports bottle spouts, and cake decorating tips, you need a dishwasher caddy. A caddy will keep those things from falling onto the dishwasher's heating element. Stack two plastic strawberry baskets together and connect them with plastic, not paper, covered twist ties. This recycled caddy lasts for many washes and keeps little items from being ruined. Retail versions are around $5.

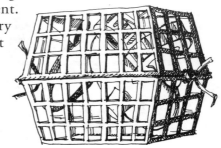

Garden Hose Blade Cover

When your garden hose has sprung one too many leaks, make a cover for your handsaw out of it. Slice an old piece of garden hose lengthwise and fit it around the exposed edge of your saw blade. This will protect the blade from chipping if dropped and keep you and all your appendages safe as well.

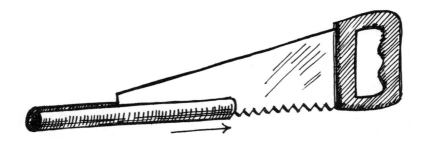

Shred It

When our gift-wrap bows are smashed beyond recognition, we don't pitch them; we shred them. Unstaple the bow to make one long line of ribbon. Place the ribbon on a table, and slide your scissors through it lengthwise several times. Or invest in an inexpensive handheld ribbon shredder (about $3). Gather several different colors of shredded ribbon, and tape to your package to give it a festive look. This is also super for gift bag stuffing. And best yet, your once useless bows are salvaged.

Lotion Leftover

Is your lotion bottle empty? Maybe not. When you think you've gotten all the lotion out of the bottle, warm up the container to *really* empty it. Place it in warm water (it can join you for a shower) or heat it briefly, with no lid, in the microwave. The warm lotion will come out more easily. You may be surprised at how much is actually left.

Toddler Toy

Fun, educational, and frugal toys are as close as your pantry shelf. My (Angie's) boys' favorite toddler toy was made out of a recycled peanut butter jar and clean juice lids. Wash a plastic jar and cut a slot of appropriate size in the top. Use clean metal juice lids from frozen juice containers for the toddler to slip in the jar. This toy exercises rotational ability, depth perception, and size evaluation skills. Store-bought toys that teach the same skills retail for over $15. Make your own—it's free!

Soap-on-a-Rope

Use up those soap slivers or tiny hotel soaps in your home. Grab a ruined nylon and make your own soap-on-a-rope. Cut off a regular pantyhose leg or use a knee-high nylon. Fill it with tiny soap bars. You can also use a mesh laundry sack. Tie the nylon or mesh sack to the shower or tub faucet. Rub your hands or washcloth over the soap ball to wash. This is great for using up small soaps and is perfect for anyone who is mobility impaired and can't chase a bar of soap around the shower floor. Retail versions run over $4.

Rag-O-Matic!

The product of the new millennium is here—the **Rag-o-matic**! With this miracle product, you can save hundreds of dollars a year. This revolutionary product is now available to households everywhere.

Simply add tap water to the **Rag-o-matic** and wipe down mirrors, counter tops, windows, and touch up floors. That's right, it's that simple. You may think a product like this would cost $29.99. But no, the fantastic **Rag-o-matic** is free and it's in your home right now! Get one of your socks that has lost its mate. Cut it lengthwise and open it up around the toe. Or take that too thin dishtowel that's just waiting to be recycled into its powerful new career as a **Rag-o-matic**. Be a homemaker of the new millennium and own a **Rag-o-matic** today!

Not available in stores. Batteries not included. All parts sold separately.

Classy Button Jewelry

Button, button, who's got the button? If you've got an old campaign button or badge, you've got the start of an elegant brooch. Take the badge and paint the top of it with colored fingernail polish. When the polish is dry, glue rhinestones or other ornaments to the top of the button. Broken earrings or other jewelry pieces can be recycled into this new treasure. With an old campaign button and a little creativity, you can make a fashionable new pin.

Plastic Bag Keeper

If your wild plastic grocery bags are making a jungle out of your pantry, recruit an empty tissue box to tame them. Mount the box to your pantry wall or keep it in a drawer. Scrunch the bags in and pop them out when needed. When the tissue box is worn out, you can toss it out and replace it for free. A hard plastic bag organizer costs $10 at the store. The tissue box organizer is also great in the classroom. Brown paper towels fit in it perfectly and it helps the kids grab just one towel at a time.

First Prize

For great kid game prizes, make awards from clean juice can lids. Hot glue the lid to a ribbon so the medal can be worn around the neck, or hot glue streamer ribbons from the bottom for a county fair look. Add star stickers to jazz them up.

Pantyhose Badminton

Don't throw away those worn out pantyhose. Use them to make a fun badminton game. Take a coat hanger and bend the hook part to make the handle. Then bend the larger part of the hanger into an oval shape. This will be the paddle. Push the oval wire into the pantyhose leg and stretch it until it's tight. Secure the pantyhose to the handle with a rubber band. Cut off the excess pantyhose. Wrap duct tape around the handle. Use a cotton ball or a balloon as the badminton shuttlecock.

Sock Cozy

If you need to keep your sports bottle cool while on the go, the answer is in your laundry room. Insulate your sports bottle with an odd sock. We've seen kids using thick thermal socks as sports bottle cozies. This is about the only use for a thermal sock in Texas. It's a challenge to see who comes up with the most unique sock. Ski socks or multicolor socks with toes receive the "cool" award. So don't pitch that odd sock, give it a new life as a sports bottle cozy.

Souper Job!

"You're a *Soup*er teacher!" and "Thanks for being a *Soup*er friend!" are clever notes to attach to this planter made from a recycled soup can. Clean out a soup can and poke small holes in the bottom. Add pebbles, potting soil, and a small starter plant. A tomato seedling in a tomato soup can is a double winner. Add clear packing tape or contact paper over the label if you are concerned that watering will cause a problem.

Scoops-R-Us

Is your sandbox in need of a new supply of scoops? Do you need one of those nifty slotted scoops for the litter box? Or a scoop for pet food or gardening? Put away your checkbook and look no further than your recycling bin.

Use a milk jug or liquid fabric softener bottle to make your new scoops. With a sharp knife, slice off the bottom at an angle. Cut slits on the scoop portion for a slotted or sifting effect. And milk jug scoops work great for a game of scoop ball.

Cheap Talk

A favorite childhood game is telephone. Here's how you can make a telephone out of an old garden hose and two tin cans. Take the garden hose and cut it to the desired length—the longer the better. Take two metal cans and punch holes in the bottom so that the opening is slightly smaller than the diameter of the hose. Squish each end of the hose into the bottom of a can until it sticks out the other end. Poke a nail across the center of each hose end, and then pull the hose back down into the can. The nail will work as a cotter pin. Stretch the hose phone between the kids' rooms or outside in the backyard. Now your kids have their own frugal phone.

Can Luminaries

Save metal cans to make luminaries. Remove the paper label. With a hammer and nail, poke holes in the side of the can to form a pattern such as a starburst. If the can bends when you poke the holes, freeze water in it to make it more sturdy. When your pattern is complete and the ice has melted, put sand in the bottom of the can and add a votive candle. A row of glowing can luminaries is beautiful at Christmastime.

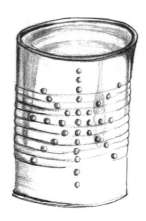

A Cheap Lift

Make a step stool out of old phone books by duct taping two books together. This also doubles as a child's booster seat.

Lost Mittens

If you've lost your mittens like the three little kittens, don't worry. With an old sweater, you can make new mittens. Trace your hand onto a piece of paper to create a pattern. Add a ½" seam allowance. Place the mitten pattern on the sleeve or waist of the sweater. The elasticized material at the sweater cuff or waist will form the cuff of the mitten. Cut out two sweater layers per mitten and sew, right sides together.

Easter Egg Candles

What do you get when you recycle candle stubs and eggshells? Easter egg candles! This is a fun way to use wilted candles to produce a clever Easter gift. Crack raw eggs at one end, empty the contents and rinse clean. Melt wax in a tin can on low heat. Add crayon pieces for color. Pastels are ideal for Easter. Put a wick recycled from a wilted candle into the eggshell, and pour in the wax. As the wax cools, the center will sink in slightly. Fill the hole with more melted wax. When cooled completely, peel off the eggshell. Easter egg candles are perfect put into a basket or given to your favorite Sunday School teacher on Easter morning.

❧

"Use it up, wear it out, make do, or do without."
—*A colonial maxim*

5

Trash to Treasure

"Hey, look what they were going to throw out at work. They said I could have it!" announced Tom (Angie's husband), walking through the door with the spindle base of an office chair.

"Great!…But isn't that going to hurt without a seat?" I asked, teasingly.

"The rest is in the truck," he answered, wondering if I was joking or if I really was that dumb. Tom had rescued a very expensive office chair that was busted in two parts. He envisioned the two parts welded together to make a $300 office chair. We promptly struck a deal with a friend who had a welder. We needed the seat and base welded together, and he needed our pickup to get a load of sand for his children's new sandbox. All of us were delighted. Our friend's children are enjoying their sandbox, and I'm writing this chapter from the comfort of a high-quality office chair.

There are three main places to find useful "trash": (1) on the job, (2) at the curb on bulky item pickup day, and (3) in a dumpster. With a scavenger's eye you can save useful things from landfill fate and put them to good use!

GREAT FINDS AT WORK

"One man's trash is another man's treasure" is especially true at a place of employment. Though it may be better said, "One company's trash is many people's treasure."

Office Equipment

In the electronic world, last year's hot-selling computer is today's dinosaur. Ditto for phone systems, fax machines, printers, and copiers. Keep a watchful eye on how your workplace deals with upgrades. Your attentiveness could net you a usable piece of equipment. Ask around to see what procedures, if any, your company has to deal with old electronics.

Obsolete Office Furniture

As new technology requires new office furniture to accommodate it; the old is typically thrown out. Most companies do not have a plan for dealing with obsolete furniture. This is good news for those of us with a scavenger nature and an inventive spirit. I changed a typewriter desk into a lovely entryway table. A friend of ours turned a solid oak, telephone operator's switchboard into a gorgeous tea cart.

Discarded Office Supplies

When a company I used to work for changed their filing system, I was given boxes of free file folders. I kept some and gave the rest to our church. The company also changed their post office box number. When I saw three 500-count boxes of envelopes being tossed out, I asked if I could have them. Our family used those envelopes for years, putting our return address label over the company's return address.

Volunteer

Another venue for finding abandoned treasures is a place you volunteer. I salvaged yards of large paper destined for the trash while helping change the bulletin boards at school. I used that paper for brightly colored gift wrap. Many teachers have given us unclaimed school supplies as a thank you for helping them pack up their room at the end of the year. One year our school moved into a new building that was already furnished with chalkboards and marker boards. They were going to throw away the ones from the old building. I snatched them up and took them directly to our church Sunday School rooms where they have been used ever since.

BULKY ITEM COLLECTION

Twice a year, my neighbors and I (Deana), participate in an event that all frugalites love. Here in Austin, it's called Bulky Item Collection Day. In Manhattan, New York, it's affectionately called Big Junk Night. Whatever your city calls it, it's a not-to-be-missed event. At the beginning of the week, residents haul their large, unwanted things to the curb. We've found remarkable items being tossed out and ridiculous reasons for their early demise—rugs, draperies, and furniture thrown out because they didn't match the new décor; good bikes abandoned because they had flat tires. Frugal folks can't wait to peruse the curbside piles to redeem still usable treasures. This creative form of recycling is commonly called "trash picking."

Still Useful Stuff

Angie and I have personally retrieved many useful things that people have thrown away. We've rescued a bucket of dinosaur toys, a Little Tykes playhouse, metal shelves, a two-drawer filing cabinet (Frugal Family Network's first office furniture), a large Rubbermaid doghouse and a scooter. The mom putting the scooter on the curb told us she was throwing it out because the kids fought over it.

New Uses

Look with a creative eye. Items that can't be used as they were originally intended can be given a new life and purpose. Angie turned an old waterbed mattress into a sandbox liner. A wicker basket can become a household trash can.

Free Parts

Sometimes you don't need the whole item, only part of it. When my dishwasher racks started leaving rust spots on my dishes, it was time to get new ones. I was able to find a dishwasher just like ours being thrown away. I took the racks out and had free replacement parts.

TIPS TO BULKY ITEM RESCUING

- Know the rules/laws concerning trash picking in your city. In most cases, trash is fair game. Just remember, don't trespass.

- If the homeowner is present, ask permission to look through their discards.

- Go outside your own neighborhood, if you'd feel more comfortable.

- There's safety and fun in numbers. Go with a friend.

- Use a truck for trash picking. You never know what large items you may find.

- Wear work gloves and work clothes.

Make a List

Make a list of things you're looking for. Just because it's free, doesn't mean you need it. If it cluttered someone else's home, it could clutter yours.

Grab It Now

If you find something you want, take it immediately. It'll probably be gone if you come back for it later. If you decide you don't need it after you get home, then you can set it out on your curb.

DUMPSTER DIVING

Dumpster diving may be considered the most radical form of turning trash into treasure. For those adventuresome souls who are willing to try it, it can yield great rewards.

College Cleanup

We first tried this three years ago. We had just finished an early morning appearance at a TV station near the university and decided to check out what the students were throwing away. The good news was the school year was ending and the dumpsters were overflowing. The bad news was, after just coming from the TV interview, we weren't exactly dressed for the task. Despite our attire, we cruised the area and quickly realized what wasteful creatures college students are. We found household items, utensils, appliances, clothing, and cleaning supplies in good or near perfect condition. We didn't have to look hard to find them. We simply perused the discards that piled up next to the full trash containers.

Changing Needs

Most "trash" is not useless garbage. Often items are tossed out because the needs of the owner or the perception of the item's usefulness have changed. While looking through a great trash stash, a fraternity boy came out with an armload of unused cleaners. We asked him why he was throwing away perfectly good supplies. He said he didn't need them anymore and had no room in his car to tote them home.

Stores, Stores, Stores

Look for greenery or ribbon in a florist's trash or large boxes for moving behind the grocery or furniture store. Other places to scrounge are dumpsters behind discount stores, motels, and construction areas. Sylvia Falconer of Greely, Colorado, wrote to say she found so much useful building material this way that she made a cat condo and had enough leftover wood for many Boy/Girl Scout projects.

Military Maneuvers

A friend of ours who lives in military on-base housing nets tremendous treasures from her neighborhood. Since families transfer frequently, they cast off many large and small items to reduce their moving load. She takes these items to the base resale shop and earns enough money to pay for their summer vacation. Civilian apartment complexes are also a good source because of the high turnover rate.

Ethics Supported

Most states do not ban dumpster diving and attorneys acknowledge an item is abandoned and has no owner when it's put in the trash. But what is legal is not necessarily ethical for everyone. Judge for yourself if this is right for you. Just remember, these things have been thrown away, not accidentally lost. The previous owner doesn't want them anymore. And every item you rescue is one less thing to crowd the landfill and one less thing you have to buy. Always respect private property and stay out of dumpsters that bear "no trespassing" signs.

What to Bring

Don't climb inside a dumpster. Bring a broom handle with a hook or curved nail on the end to poke through the trash and snag the item of your desire. Wear gloves, long pants and sleeves, and closed toe shoes to protect yourself. Bring along a garbage bag to throw your loot into.

Timing

Go just before dusk. It will be light enough to see, businesses will have just closed and set out fresh items, and you'll feel braver than you would in broad daylight.

Pass on the Pastries

Don't eat food found in the dumpster. Though some brave frugalites do consume food in its original, unopened packaging, we do not recommend it.

"Simplify. Simplify."
—Henry David Thoreau

6

Garage Sale Gold Mine

We've all heard of the woman who buys a piece of junk at a yard sale for 25¢ and later discovers it's a museum-quality artifact worth a small fortune. That may happen to some, but it hasn't happened to us, but that's OK. The true treasure of a garage sale is buying things for next to nothing and never paying full retail price. Over the years we've saved hundreds of dollars by shopping at garage sales rather than heading to the store. Whether you call it a garage sale, tag sale, or rummage sale, the best place to find just about anything at true tightwad prices is a short Saturday morning drive from your front door.

Toys

Angie has found name-brand toys such as Hot Wheels® Double Barrel Racetrack and Discovery Toys Marbleworks® for $1 each. These toys were *very* gently used, had all their parts, and were in the original boxes. Toys like these make excellent gifts for your children. Yes, our kids have grown up with garage sale gifts. They don't notice and don't care if the toy was in the original plastic wrapping. They're only interested in playing with it as soon as the gift wrapping is off. Played with a little or a lot, you can never play all the fun out of it.

Kid's Clothes

Children's clothing is an excellent buy at garage sales. Kids grow through clothes and shoes so quickly that many items can be found in great condition. Expect to pay only 25–50¢ for kid's clothes. Suits, coats, dress shoes, or other specialty items may go for $1 or $2. If clothes are only slightly worn, it may be an indication that the garment is durable enough to go a second round with another family. Angie has been so successful dressing her boys from garage sales finds that over the years the only things she has had to buy at the store were socks. Any garment from a garage sale can be made germ-free by washing in hot water of 120°F or higher.

Designer Kids

If you are reluctant to buy kid's clothes at yard sales, examine your attitude toward garage sale garments. Does a four year old really need designer clothes to make mud pies? The status symbol on his shirt doesn't matter to him and his playmates. If the label does matter to you, be assured we've found plenty of gently used, designer duds at garage sales. Angie recently paid 50¢ for a Ralph Lauren Polo shirt for Timothy. The mall price would have been $35.95! Our kids are well dressed and have never looked shabby.

Adult Clothes

Clothing for men and women is as abundant as children's clothes, and just as fantastically priced. Buy classic styles that look good on you and won't become tomorrow's fads. Fads are bad buys at any price. Check for stains, missing buttons, or broken zippers.

Decorating

Flea market decorating, known as "shabby chic," is very popular. But there's no reason to pay extra for "distressed" furniture; just buy stuff at garage sales. You can also find near perfect furnishings. I (Deana) bought an Ethan Allen solid wood side table for $25 that was in excellent condition. Pictures, frames, china, lamps, and home accessories are all abundant and reasonably priced at yard sales. Almost all the Americana accessories in my son's room are from garage sales.

Garage Sale Guarantees

Things are sold at garage sales "as is." There are no guarantees given on most items. But did you know some products have lifetime guarantees? You don't have to be the original buyer to receive it. Tupperware will replace any cracked piece. Any Tupperware dealer can handle the exchange for you. We've done this and used the new pieces as gifts. Farberware, Chicago Cutlery, and Craftsman tools also have lifetime guarantees. Angie's brother Jerry bought a broken Craftsman socket wrench at a garage sale for 50¢. He took it to Sears, and they replaced it with a new $75 wrench. Consult the company to learn of any limitations and how to receive a new product.

Take a Risk

In addition to bargain prices, you also have the comfort of knowing your financial risk is low at a garage sale. I bought my daughter, Katie, a cool jean jacket at a garage sale for just $2. At least I thought it was cool. Unfortunately, she hated it. But since it was bought at a garage sale, my loss was minimal. If I had bought it at the store and she had worn it a few times, I couldn't have returned it. I would have been stuck with a purchase ten times as expensive as the garage sale buy.

Be Prepared

When you go to garage sales, be prepared. Bring cash in small bills and change in a fanny pack or other type of hands-free container. Make a list of the items you are looking for, including the size and color for clothes. Carry a measuring tape, especially if you are shopping for window coverings or furniture. Pack a snack and a jacket for inclement weather. Also include paper sacks or a sheet to hide items you want to give as gifts.

New Attitude

One of the most important things to bring to a garage sale is a new attitude toward shopping. If you go to a garage sale with a retail attitude—expecting to find many items, all in perfect condition and in the right size and color for you—you're bound to be disappointed. Treat a garage sale as an adventure or treasure hunt.

Where to Go

Scan the newspaper's Friday classified section to see where garage sales are clustered and plan your route accordingly. I use a well-worn map and circle the garage sale sites. Numbering the stops helps me plan the most efficient route. I've chosen an older neighborhood as my regular garage sale haunt. Many of these homes are being renovated by young professionals, and they often have building materials for sale. Since we are slowly remodeling our home, I find many useful items.

Group Garage Sales

Every year I tingle with excitement as I see St. Catherine's Catholic Church setting up for their huge annual garage sale. We love going to garage sales put on by neighborhoods, churches, clubs, and sports organizations. Group sales offer more selection with less running around. It's good to go with a friend. Another pair of eyes might spot something you overlooked among the vast merchandise.

Haggle

Some people shy away from garage sales because they don't like haggling over prices. If you don't want to haggle, then don't. Garage sale prices will still be cheaper than retail, even without dickering. If you are a novice at bargaining, then start with a question, such as, "How much do you want for this?" or "Would you take 50¢ for this?" Those questions might save you up to 50 percent off the price and the only thing you risk is hearing "no" in response. If you find the seller inflexible and the prices too high, just move on. There's always another garage sale around the corner.

Go Early

If you arrive at a garage sale just as the signs are going up, you're sure to get the best selection. The trade-off is firm prices. Sellers won't make deals since they know a parade of other buyers is following you. Arriving early is important if you're looking for furniture or appliances. There are fewer of these items, and they will be scooped up quickly. Resale shop owners are out early, buying truckloads of furniture and appliances for their businesses.

Go Late

Around noon or later, garage sale hosts are ready to pack up and call it a day. They are willing to get rid of their stuff at almost any price. Some will begin to offer "fill-a-bag-for-a-dollar," just to avoid hauling it back into the house. You won't find the best selection, but the prices can't be beat.

Ask for Something

If you're hoping to find a little red wagon at a garage sale, but you don't see one, ask for it. I've seen people go into their houses and bring out the requested item and sell it on the spot. Sometimes other shoppers will overhear your request and tell you of a garage sale that has that item.

Free Box

Many garage sales set out a box of items that they are giving away for free. You might think that there will be nothing of value in this box, but you would be surprised. Check out this box first. You can't beat the price!

Double Your Efforts

Give a list of things you're looking for to your garage sale friends. They'll take your list with them to the sales they go to, essentially doubling your efforts. Include details about the color, size, and top price you'd pay for the item. Be sure to hunt for their requested items also.

Buy Parts

Sometimes a garage sale item is valuable for its parts. I've bought an absolutely hideous blouse in order to get a set of great buttons. Angie's Boggle game was missing a letter "E" cube. She found a Boggle game at a garage sale for 50¢ and was able to replace her missing part. And don't pass up that ugly yellow lamp. The shade may be just what you need for your shadeless lamp.

Stay Safe

Shop a neighborhood you're familiar with. You'll navigate faster and stay out of unknown territory. Go with a friend. It's more fun. Leave the kids at home. You won't have to worry about them, and you'll be a more focused shopper. Don't enter anyone's home alone.

You Bought What?

You can buy anything at a garage sale. I once saw rocks for sale. Not landscape stones, not mineral specimens, just rocks. I can't remember what they were priced. I just remember trying not to laugh. Though I haven't bought rocks, I have bought some things you may not think to look for, such as Christmas wrapping paper, school supplies, and household cleaners. Angie regularly buys bars of soap for her family. She finds enough soap at garage sales that she doesn't have to buy any at the store.

Though we've never found a priceless museum piece, we know garage sales are worth it. The thrill of finding just what we're looking for at rock-bottom prices is more valuable to us than a museum full of treasures.

❧

"My riches consist not in the extent of my possessions, but in the fewness of my wants.
—J. Brotherton

Kids Korner: Raising Kids for Less

Recently, we read an estimate that it costs parents over $300,000 to raise a child from birth through high school. We think that figure is inflated, and we're happy to say we know we can raise children for less. Long ago frugal families learned smart ways to clothe, play with, and provide for their children without a hefty price tag.

Pass-Along Network

Developing a network with other frugal families to exchange clothes, household goods, and various sundries is by far the most powerful tool we've used to provide for our families. I (Angie) have given and received bicycles, appliances, clothing, toys, and food. Once you are known as someone who gives and receives graciously, the abundance will begin to flow. If you are not currently in a pass-along network or if you want to beef up the connections you currently have, use the Share-Accept-Ask principle:

Share First: Take a stack of outgrown clothing and give it to another family. I approach larger families first as their need is greater and they've already developed an appreciation for gently used things. Sharing first is a good way to start a new connection.

Accept Graciously: Accept all things given to you graciously. Most people are happy to give their no-longer-needed items to another family who will use them. If you reject their offer, you rob the giver of the blessing of giving. You also dry up the connection for future things. I once offered a new mother some toddler clothes. She decided not to accept the clothing since they were not her preferred brand and were not her son's "colors." Though I respected her decision, since then I've looked elsewhere when passing along my boys' clothing. If you are given something, but can't use it all, glean what is useful to your family, and then pass the extra on to someone else.

Ask: Let others know what you are searching for. When Adam outgrew his bicycle, I told friends of our quest for a larger bike. Within a few days, a neighbor called to say we could have the bicycle their son had outgrown. By using the Share-Accept-Ask principle, you will have most needs and many wants satisfied through an informal network of fellow frugal families.

Socks for All
Buy only one style of socks for your kids. That way when one is lost, there is always another to match. Basic white works well for boys and girls.

Best Foot Forward
When your kids outgrow their footed pajamas, don't buy new ones. Cut off the feet and attach tube socks to give their jammies a longer life.

Confetti Eggs
One of my most enjoyable discoveries when I became a Texan was confetti eggs! Also known as cascarones, these simple eggshells filled with confetti are a blast of entertainment. Children and adults crack them over each other's heads, releasing the confetti, in a flurry of tag-style excitement. Best yet, these little jewels are completely free to make! Make a small

opening in the end of a raw egg and let the inside slip out. Rinse the shell with water (add a drop of bleach if you're concerned about germs) and let it dry. Dye the eggshells and decorate them with markers and stickers. Fill them with "confetti" such as punches from a three-hole punch, shredded paper, or imported Florida chads. Glue a small piece of tissue paper or old paper  streamer over the opening. It's confetti mayhem when the kids get an egg in each hand and chase each other around the yard. The eggshells are good for your lawn and the small paper pieces will compost quickly.

Snow Show

For surefire winter fun, let the kids paint pictures in the snow. This is inexpensive creative fun. Fill empty plastic squeeze bottles (like ketchup) with food coloring and cold water to make the snow paint. Start with primary colors and blend them to create beautiful pictures in the snow.

Marbles, Yo-Yos, and Puppets

In our electronic world, marbles, yo-yos, and puppets may seem too pale, but unplug the kids and try these classic frugal pastimes. When I taught my kids how to play marbles, they loved it. Now they are always on the hunt for the perfect shooter. Remember the yo-yo craze of the 1970s? Teach your kids tricks you remember. And puppets! I can't say enough about them. Set up a makeshift puppet stage out of an accordion-folded sewing board or a couple of chairs covered with a sheet. Have the kids act out skits with their stuffed animals or make puppets out of socks.

Party Piñatas

Piñatas are a standard at our parties. This wonderful Mexican tradition offers lots of frugal fun if done the right way. A store-bought piñata stuffed with expensive chocolates easily costs over

$20. However, we use frugal resourcefulness and make a piñata for little cash. I buy unused piñatas at garage sales for $1 or less. I stuff the piñata with trinkets and small toys I've accumulated throughout the year. Small plastic toys from the doctor's office, the brightly colored key rings from our insurance agent, and free pencils and balloons from the bank work well. After that, I add a couple bags of clearance-sale candy that I've stashed away in our freezer. The piñata is the grand finale at our parties. The kids love it, and it's a blast of fun for usually less than $2.

Make Your Own Piñata

Making a piñata is messy frugal fun. Create the simplest form with balloons. (Odd balloon shapes and lightweight cardboard, like toilet paper tubes, can be combined to form a variety of characters and objects.) Blow up a balloon as large as possible. Then make a paste of flour and water. I've also used leftover plaster mix I got from a garage sale "Free Box." Make the mixture slightly thinner than oatmeal. Dip 1"-wide newspaper strips in the mixture and begin laying wet paper over the balloon. Apply three layers and let them dry. Do this three times for a total of nine layers. Thread a wire hanger through the top to make a hook to attach the rope. Decorate when dry. We've used leftover house paint, streamers, and fringed paper—anything that's free. Cut a flap on one side of the piñata, pop the balloon, and stuff with treats. A piñata is a recycler's dream! Try one at your next party and have a smashing good time.

Play with Your Food

Don't buy an overpriced decorated cake at the store, look in your toy box instead. Add small clean toys to a frosted cake. It's a fast and frugal decoration.

Go Crackers

To make a birthday cake with a zoo theme, place animal crackers on top and around the sides of the cake.

Better Band-Aids

Rather than buying expensive bandages in multi-packs to get tiny toddler Band-Aids, purchase the regular size and cut them in half lengthwise. You get a better Band-Aid with longer adhesive strips and the regular size is cheaper. That's twice as many Band-Aids for less money!

Egg-ceptional Flowers and Critters

There are tons of fun free things to create from egg cartons.

Bouquet of Tulips: Cut an individual eggcup from the carton. Trim the sides to make rounded or pointed petals. Insert a green straw or pipe cleaner through the bottom of the cup to form a stem. If you are using gray pressed paper cartons, paint the cups bright colors. Add construction paper leaves to the stem to finish the bouquet.

Spider: Cut a cup from the carton and attach eight pipe cleaner segments or twist ties for legs. Draw on eyes and a smile.

Caterpillar: Cut a row of four eggcups off of the carton. Attach twist ties for antennae. Add a happy face.

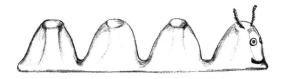

Process over Product

The most important aspect of play is the process not the product. Let your children enjoy the process of painting rather than being concerned about the final picture. By using this approach, you will foster a child who loves to learn, explore, and create.

Animal Tub Time

Hand wash stuffed animals by letting your kids take them into the tub with them. They will both get clean and have fun at the same time. You'll save the time and water you would have spent washing the stuffed animals.

Essential Baby Equipment

Advertising says we must buy all the latest, greatest stuff to be "good" parents. We can tell you from experience that we didn't need, nor ever use, most of it. Here is the essential equipment that most families need.

Car Seat: Having and using a safe car seat is a must, and there is no financial reason not to have one. Most hospitals give out free infant seats for newborns. These are no-frills seats but they are safe. Some insurance companies offer a free car seat program or free exchanges for recalled car seats. Take advantage of car seat safety checks sponsored by the police, fire, or ambulance departments. Friends of ours received new car seats free when theirs didn't pass inspection.

Crib: Strong crib manufacturing guidelines were set in 1973. The space between the slates was reduced to 2⅜″ along with other regulations. These rules were developed to eliminate the infant deaths that were occurring due to entrapment. Only use a crib that is current on all safety requirements.

High Chair: A high chair is a borderline necessity, but both Deana and I agree that life would have been more difficult without it. When shopping for a high chair, look for a safe and easy-to-manipulate tray, easy-to-clean seat, and legs that are sturdy and slide along the floor.

Stroller: A stroller will earn its keep quickly. Select one with washable seats, built-in storage compartment, and, for us taller parents, a handle that extends to a comfortable height.

Nonessentials: For baby equipment such as an infant swing, backpack, snuggly, or walker, borrow them from a friend to try them out first. My boys screamed when they were in a swing, backpack, snuggly—well, you get the picture. If after "test-driving" it, you find a piece of equipment that fits your child's temperament, then it may be worth the investment.

Check for Recalls

When buying secondhand or receiving pass-along baby equipment, call the Consumer Product Safety Commission at 1-800-638-2772 to check for recalls. They also have a free publication called "The Safe Nursery."

Belts-R-Us

Newsletter subscriber Deanna Bortner of Austin, Texas, wrote to say she discovered a solution to finding belts for her boys. She buys the narrow adult belts at garage sales, cuts them to the right length, and then punches new holes. Mrs. Bortner also takes her older son's belt, which has cracked from bending it in the same spot, trims the frayed edges, and punches new holes to fit her younger son.

High Security

To keep your toddler from slipping out of his high chair, put a small rubber bath or sink mat on the seat.

Dress-Up Box

A fun way to prompt imaginary play in kids for free is with a dress-up box. Our box contains Tom's old Air Force uniform, a graduation gown, hats, vests, a Superman cape, and a pair of cowboy boots. Deana includes old bridesmaid dresses in her kids' box as well as elbow length gloves and ballerina tutus. Fill your dress-up box with these ideas or any fun garage sale finds. Dramatic or imaginary play is essential for good writing skills and social development.

Clever Costumes

Most families need costumes at one time or another. But don't make a trip to an expensive costume shop; check what is free in your home first. A cardboard box has endless costume possibilities. Cut a hole for the head on the top, cut two arm holes on the side, and cut out the bottom for the legs.

Then get creative! To turn two people into a pair of dice, paint the sides of each box white or cover with paper. Add the appropriate dots. To become a gift, cover a box with Christmas wrap and add a big red bow on your head. A rectangular box can be painted as a refrigerator, a candy bar, or a TV remote.

White sheets are always a perfect costume standby. Cut a hole for the head and tie up the bottom ends of the sheet just below the waist. Stuff with plastic grocery bags and you're a marshmallow or a cotton ball. Add silver Christmas garland to the bottom and you are a cloud with a silver lining. My sister Betty won a creative costume prize for the cloud idea.

Can you guess what this costume is? A sheet of paper with a large letter P on it is draped over a person with black paint around one eye. Any guesses? It's a black-eyed pea!

Homemade Play Dough

Homemade play dough is far superior to store-bought and costs less than 40¢ to make. The consistency is better and it's more versatile as you can add color and scent. Here's my favorite recipe:

2	cups flour
1	cup salt
2	cups water
2	tablespoons oil
4	teaspoons cream of tartar

Mix all ingredients together on low heat until the consistency is like mashed potatoes. Cool and refrigerate overnight. Add food coloring and scent (flavoring like coconut, lemon, or strawberry) when cooled.

Diaper Dilemma

No matter how you calculate it, cloth diapers are cheaper than disposable ones, hands down. Or should that be bottoms down? Even comparing store-brand disposable diapers against utility costs, cloth diapers will save you about $400 per child per year. Though mothers frequently lament about the cost of disposable diapers, few try to use cloth because of strongly held misconceptions. Here are some of the most frequently voiced objections:

"I can't go out of the house and use cloth diapers."

Sure you can. There is no difference in finding a place to change a cloth diaper in public versus a disposable one. Just slip the used cloth diaper into doubled plastic grocery bags.

"What if they poop?"

Yes, "poop happens." If you are near a restroom, dump the solids in the toilet, and then wrap up the diaper in double plastic grocery bags.

"My hands will get wet changing a cloth diaper."

Then wash your hands. You would do this after changing a disposable diaper anyway.

"What about the cost of buying cloth diapers."

I (Angie) received two dozen cloth diapers as a baby shower gift. I bought some extras at garage sales. Diapers cost about $10 a dozen brand new.

"Won't cloth diapers soaking in a pail of water get smelly?"

No worse than a trashcan of disposable diapers. Adding baking soda or vinegar to the water will help.

"Won't this cause a lot of laundry?"

About one extra load per week will be required. But even the extra laundry cost is cheaper than a package of diapers.

"But all that folding!"

Why fold? Use prefolded diapers. Once they come out of the dryer, toss them in a basket and use from there. This isn't a dress shirt; it's a diaper. Wrinkles are allowed.

"Won't my child get diaper rash?"

The only time my boys had diaper rash was when they had been in disposable diapers. It was never a problem in cloth diapers. Other mothers have had similar experiences.

There are places that require disposable diapers such as day care centers. Disposables will hold more wetness for a longer period of time making overnight use a good option. But for daily use, cloth diapers can't be beat.

Baby Wipes

To make less expensive homemade baby wipes, cut a roll of paper towels in half widthwise. A serrated knife will cut best. Separate the towels into individual wipes and place in a sealable container. Mix 1 tablespoon of baby bath or shampoo with ½ tablespoon of baby oil into 2 cups of water. Pour the mixture over the paper towels in the container and keep sealed. For free wipes, cut up old T-shirts or odd socks and just wet them with water. If you have an abundance of them, you can throw them away after using just like disposables, or toss them in the wash with cloth diapers.

"Mommy, sometimes you just need to relax a little bit and make mud pies."
—Josie Trager, age 3

SOS:
Save on Sports

It was the last inning of the T-ball finals and our (Angie and Tom's) five-year-old son, Timothy, was on second base. At the crack of the bat, Timothy shot a beeline for third and headed toward home.

Two yards from home plate, Timothy stopped. Completely oblivious to the excited shouting of the crowd, he bent over to examine a unique rock. After a few excruciatingly long seconds, Timothy slipped the rock into his pocket and continued strolling toward home without a care in the world. He casually stepped on home plate a split second before the ball landed in the catcher's mitt. "Safe!" the umpire hollered. The crowd burst into cheers and laughter while a calm Timothy returned to the bench.

Our families have been involved in baseball, soccer, basketball, karate, swimming, tennis, gymnastics, weightlifting, and aerobics. We've found many strategies that allow us to participate in sports without karate chopping our wallets.

Equipment

Pick a sport that requires less equipment or less costly equipment. A good pair of shoes is all you need for most track-and-field events, while football requires pads, helmet, mouth guard, and a myriad of other protective gear. If you are deciding between two sports that will be enjoyed equally, factor the cost of equipment into your decision.

Find Frugal Friends

Connect with friends who have a child older than yours who was in the same sport. Ask if you may buy, use, or barter for their child's outgrown equipment. Keep in mind many sporting goods are unisex like baseball gloves, soccer shin guards, and cleats. I met a family at church whose older son went to the same karate school as the one in which Timothy is enrolled. I've arranged to receive their son's uniform when Timothy outgrows his. If you don't know of anyone, ask coaches if they can recommend someone from a previous season.

Free Exchange Day

Our soccer league has a Free Exchange Day when parents bring their kids' outgrown equipment to trade and barter with other parents. Ask if your sports association has something similar. If not, offer to start one!

Lost and Found

The lost and found box from last year may hold just what you need. Ask the sports league what they do with lost and found items. They may be happy to let you have something from last year's box.

Garage Sales

We have bought bats, gloves, balls, soccer goals, and many other pieces of equipment at garage sales for pennies on the dollar. Watch for fundraising garage sales, especially ones sponsored by other sports teams. Tom was reluctantly dragged to a garage sale one Saturday morning and hit the jackpot on baseball bats. Because he knew the brands and bat weight requirements for the different team levels, he was able to pick up several high-quality bats for a few dollars.

Consignment Shops

Look in your yellow pages under "Sports equipment" or "Consignment/Resale" to find consignment stores in your area. The merchandise in these shops is previously owned but often in good condition. The price can't beat a garage sale but is generally 50 percent less than full retail price. Deana outfitted her son with used golf equipment this way and saved a bundle.

Uniforms

Most uniforms are issued new each season. With our local baseball teams, however, only the shirt is included with the participation fee. Pants, socks, and shoes must be bought personally. When my (Angie's) sons, Timothy and Adam, were in T-ball, they wore regular gray sweatpants rather than baseball pants. Instead of $20 cleats and $4 baseball socks, they wore cleats I got at a garage sale for 50¢ and regular socks. Find out which uniform parts are included with the league fee and which you will need to buy separately. Then substitute some of the things for which you're responsible with clothing you already have.

Stay Organized

Label uniforms and equipment the minute you get them. It's expensive and frustrating to replace lost items. Designate a space for the kids' sports equipment. A basket by the back door will save a lot of headaches when it's time to run to practice.

A Homemade Field

Make boundary markers with recycled milk jugs or bleach bottles. Fill them halfway with sand and set on the corners of your "field." Remnant carpet squares make good bases.

Sneaky Wallet Snatchers

Be aware of sports that have ongoing hidden costs like buying patches for achievement levels or paying for skills testing. Forced fundraising, team snacks, coaches' gifts, end-of-season parties, trophies, and tournament travel can add up, so count them in when you decide to embark on a particular sport.

Fees

It is more difficult to save on registration fees because they are set by sports leagues and are usually nonnegotiable. Occasionally, however, fees are waived for the children of coaches and administrative helpers. If you are willing, you may be able to volunteer your time in exchange for the registration fee. Also, some leagues have reduced fees or scholarships for low-income families or foster children.

Creativity Goes a Long Way

Think of creative ways to meet the needs of your own situation. After a couple practice sessions in Pony League baseball, we discovered a brilliant truth of physics: Timothy's head is a magnet for baseballs. Before the season even started, Timothy resigned his baseball career for basketball, because in his words, "Mom, the ball is softer." Our youngest son, Adam, decided at the last minute he wanted to play baseball. With one phone call the league was willing to swap Timothy's registration fee for Adam's. All I had to do was ask.

Bags

Keep plastic grocery bags in your car to wrap muddy sports shoes and clothes. This will save your car's interior.

To Buy or Not to Buy

Evaluate what needs to be purchased and what doesn't. Tom was assistant coach for our son's T-ball team. Some assistant coaches purchased $18 team shirts for themselves, so they would match their boys' shirts. Tom opted to wear a red T-shirt he already had, which looked perfect in the sea of Cardinals' shirts.

Instant Sports Drink

Keep recycled water bottles in the freezer. Fill them halfway with water and freeze. When it's time to go to practice or the game, fill it the rest of the way with water. The ice will slowly melt giving your athlete a cold drink. It's much cheaper than a sports drink.

Carpool

Carpooling with teammates to games and practices can cut your gas bill in half.

You Ought to Be in Pictures

Take your own photos of the team and your sports star instead of buying expensive professional photo packages. Have your best picture duplicated at the local photo center to give to Grandma and friends. If you are photographically challenged, save money and buy only the team photo.

The Playbook

Coaches can make a reusable playbook out of an old cookie sheet and magnets. Use a permanent marker or tape to draw the lines of the field or court on the cookie sheet. Use recycled magnets to show players or positions.

Tame the Smell

Smelly athletic shoes can be deodorized with a simple sprinkle of baking soda. For extra tough odor, wrap the shoes in a plastic bag and place them in the freezer overnight.

Change into Street Shoes

Good athletic shoes can be expensive. To make yours last longer, wear them only for sports. After the game, change into street shoes. Running errands in your athletic shoes all day will wear them out faster.

Keep Shoes Dry

Loosen the laces and pull the tongue back to allow air to circulate into the shoes. Shoes that stay damp will develop fiber-rotting mildew.

Blister Blaster

Deana's husband, Joe, ran in cross-country races while in high school. He learned that rubbing a dry bar of soap on your socks can prevent blisters. The soap leaves a waxy residue on the sock, resulting in less friction between your foot and the shoe.

Homemade Shin Protectors

Cut the feet off holey socks to make leggings that work well under shin guards. This way you'll prevent rubbing without the discomfort of wearing two pairs of socks.

ૐ

"Playing golf the other day, I broke seventy. That's a lot of golf clubs."
—Henny Youngman

Frugal Fido: Saving Money on Pet Care

My (Angie's) brother Jerry is a truck driver and has a teacup poodle named Smokey that rides with him. Smokey is a great companion, just the right size and a super little alarm system as well. When we were visiting recently, Jerry said he had paid $300 for Smokey. Tom laughed and said, "Hey, we only paid $30 for our dog and he's ten times bigger!"

A pet can be a blessing to your family without being a huge drain on your wallet. Here are some tips to reduce pet costs and still have a healthy, happy companion.

The Right Pet for You

Select an animal that is right for you and your lifestyle. If you live in an apartment and are often gone, fish, lizards, or turtles may be the right match. A large working dog like a shepherd or collie would be right at home in the country. Selecting the right animal will save you money and frustration. Trying to make something work that wasn't the correct fit from the beginning is always costly.

Where to Get a Pet

There are plenty of pets available free from a variety of sources. All but one of our pets have been strays we've adopted (or they've adopted us). Since our home is in the country it is a magnet for drive-by dumping of unwanted pets. But they've all been a joy to us and were certainly the right price. If you don't have an ample supply of strays near you, call me and you can have some of mine (just kidding). Check the pet shop bulletin boards or call a veterinarian. They usually know of pets that need a good home. Your local animal shelter has many loving pets available. Adoption fees and other requirements can be stringent so read all the regulations prior to committing.

Don't let image issues strangle your wallet. If you must have a pedigreed dog because you are going to breed it, show it, or need a purebred hunting dog, then going to a breeder may be right for you. But if you just need a healthy family pet, skip the registered papers, and get a loving animal. Our best pets have been mutts.

Try It before You Buy It

If you're not sure you want to get a pet, offer to pet-sit first. This will let you and your children see what is involved in caring for a pet. Classroom animals are always in need of babysitting during school holidays. Or offer to pet-sit while your neighbors are away.

Pet Treats

Freeze meat trimmings or table scraps for pet treats. We let them thaw slightly and use them as rewards during training.

Tug-o-War

To keep your dog or puppy from nipping at your clothes, make a free tug-o-war toy. Cut one leg off an old pair of denim or corduroy jeans. Slice the cut leg piece into three strips and braid tightly. Knot the ends several times to secure the strips. By playing tug-o-war with your dog, it will help satisfy his need to bite, chew, and tug.

Food Dishes

A recycled plastic bowl makes a good pet dish and is free. It's also easily replaced if Fido decides to use it as a chew toy.

Staked Pet Dish

If your outdoor dog keeps knocking over his food or water dish, then stake it! Recycle an old bundt pan or buy one at a garage sale and drive a stake down through the center opening. This will keep the dish steady, preventing your dog from spilling food. It's also easy to empty and clean. Just slide the dish over the stake to rinse and refill.

Christmas Tin Storage

Use the large decorative popcorn tin you got for Christmas to store pet food. You can put your pretty tin to practical use and have an attractive container for pet food, all for free.

Pet Scoop

Cut the bottom off of a mouthwash bottle at an angle to make the perfect pet food scoop. The spout, with the lid on, makes a good handle. Deana uses a recycled plastic cup that holds the exact amount of food that Sparky needs. This helps their once overweight dog to keep trim and healthy. (See chapter 4 for more pet scoop ideas.)

Water Wisdom

If you will be gone overnight, make sure your pets have plenty of water. Put a large chunk of ice in their water bowl. The ice will slowly melt, supplying them with fresh water while you are gone. Set the bowl in a pie plate to catch over-flow. No need to buy an automatic water dispenser from the pet store.

Gourmet Generic Cat Food

When you open a can of tuna, pour the tuna liquid over the dry cat food. It makes ordinary dry cat food taste like gourmet—or so the cats tell me.

Cat Scratching Post

Make a cat scratching post for free. Use scrap lumber to make a base with a simple pole. Cover it with carpet scraps from discontinued sample books. Home improvement stores and flooring companies will give them to people who ask. The simplest scratching posts cost over $20 in the pet store; yours is free.

Kitty Litter

If you live on sandy soil, instead of buying cat litter, just fill the litter box with clean sand from the outside. It costs nothing, is always available, and works well. If you live on rocky rather than sandy soil, stretch your cat's litter by adding shredded paper, hole punches, or cedar shavings. Also put a towel or rug in front of the litter box so that any sand or litter left on the cat's paws will drop off onto the rug and not into your carpet.

Cat Toys

Entertain the kids and save on cat toys at the same time. Have the kids blow bubbles outside. Children love playing with bubbles and cats love chasing them. For other fun cat toys, use things you have on hand. Our cat loves chasing a crunched ball of paper. We also put two little bells in a plastic Easter egg. She loves batting it around.

Destructo-pet

To deter pets from chewing on electrical cords, rub a bar of soap on the cords. The soap smell and taste will keep your pets from harming themselves and ruining your electronics. If your cat is scratching the furniture legs, rub lemon leaves on the wood. Cats dislike this smell and will stay away.

Great Grooming

Save money by grooming your pet yourself. To learn how, watch a pet groomer closely and ask questions. If you're still hesitant to try it at home, ask the groomer if they rent grooming bays. You will get the convenience of the facility and tools and some expert advice as well.

Pet or People Products

Many products that are marketed for pets are similar to people products, but sell at a premium price. For example, pet hair clippers cost $65, but people hair clippers are only $20. As far as we can tell, there isn't any significant difference. Also, pet pillows are overpriced compared to recycling a people pillow instead.

Pooper Scooper

If you have to scoop the poop, get plastic instead of paper at the grocery store. When Deana takes Sparky for a walk in their suburban neighborhood, she brings along a double sacked plastic grocery bag. She inverts the bag over her hand and uses it for scooping and discarding. The plastic sleeves around newspapers work well too. When Deana told me this tip, I was so thankful to live in the country where my 120-pound German shepherd/Border collie can make any of our five acres his outhouse.

Doggie Duds

In winter, some small house pets get cold easily. Newsletter subscriber Gloria Miller from Lee's Summit, Missouri, uses this alternative to buying expensive doggie sweaters. Get a toddler or baby sweater from a thrift shop or hand-me-downs and cut off the sleeves about two inches from the shoulders. Hem the sleeves and put a drawstring around the waist. The homemade sweater works as well as an expensive store-bought one.

Dog Training

A well-trained dog will reward you many times over for your efforts. But you don't need to spend top dollar to train your pooch. Begin by checking out a book or video from your library. Matthew Margolis, "Uncle Matty," is a well-known dog trainer and has a series of videotapes on dog training. Also surf to your local Public Broadcasting Service (PBS) station's website. Look on their programming schedule for dog training shows. I've watched many of these and they are helpful.

You don't need to buy special training stuff. When we began training our dog, we bought an expensive six-foot, leather training leash because, well, that's what the video told us to do. Once common sense flew back into my brain, I realized the five-and-a-half foot leash we already had would work just fine. I took the pricey leather leash back to the store the next day.

Vaccinate Your Pet Yourself

Did you know in most states you can vaccinate your dogs and cats yourself? Multi-vaccines can be purchased at a farm and ranch store or pet supply shop. I pay $3.97 for the cat vaccine. The same vaccine at the vet ran over $85! By law, only vets may administer rabies shots. Call your local animal shelter and ask if they know of a low-cost clinic for rabies shots. And don't feel squeamish about giving your pup a shot. As we say in our workshops, "Ladies, if you are tough enough to have a baby, you can certainly vaccinate your pet!"

Pet Carrier

Save money by making your own pet carrier. Take two plastic laundry baskets and stack them, top sides together. Then tie them shut. After the trip to the vet, the laundry baskets can still be used for their original purpose. This also saves on the storage space the infrequently used pet carrier takes up in your garage. Some veterinarians give away free cardboard pet carriers. Ask if these are available.

Spay and Neuter

To find low-cost and quality spay and neuter services, call your local animal shelter and ask them for recommendations. Many cities have Animal Trustee chapters that have economical neuter clinics. We've had all our pets neutered through them and have had excellent results. If you live near a college of veterinary or animal science, call to see if they spay and neuter at reduced rates.

Save the Seed

Toss your bag of birdseed in the freezer for four days when you first get it. This will kill the moth larva that are usually in with the seed. By keeping moths from hatching, you save your home from moth infestation and the damage they can cause.

Better Bird Feed

Our friend Dolores Gilligan, *Country's Calling* editor, says mesh bags from fruits or vegetables can be used as a bird feeder. Filled with suet, it's simple and inexpensive.

Useful Pets

Another approach to raising pets is choosing animals that produce a product. If your neighborhood allows, try raising a milking goat or a few chickens. A milking goat will provide fresh milk daily and do lawn mowing on the side. And chickens lay an egg about every thirty-six hours. A friend of ours tried raising hens on their "ranchette." After several months of the hens not laying eggs, she tried switching chicken feed, changing their daily schedule, and even redesigning the chicken coop. At long last she found out that she had purchased menopausal chickens. Do your research before embarking on livestock farming and enjoy the adventure.

Large Animals

If you have a passion for large animals like horses but your living space or budget doesn't permit such a financial obligation, try these ideas. Volunteer to be a warm-up rider at a stable. Or get a part-time or full-time job working with horses at a stable or veterinary clinic. Offer to "horse-sit" for ranchers while they are away. When I was growing up, my family rarely left home overnight, as it was difficult to find someone who would take on the daily livestock chores. You can still have all the enjoyment of these lovely animals without the great expense that goes with them.

"Dogs feel very strongly that they should always go with you in the car, in case the need should arise for them to bark violently at nothing right in your ear."
—Dave Barry

Thrifty Travel: Frugal Family Vacations

The words "family vacation" can strike terror in even the stoutest heart. We (Zalewskis) experienced our first family vacation a few years ago when we went to South Dakota. The trip was akin to a Chevy Chase *Vacation* movie. We can laugh about it now. Our campsite was mosquito infested, and it rained for thirty-six hours straight. Around 4 A.M., rain began leaking into our tent. In our scramble for dryer ground, Tom broke a crown. So there I am, trying to piece it together in his mouth, with Polygrip . . . in the dark . . . in the van . . . with a flashlight. And of course, Adam threw up in the van on the way back. It's an unwritten rule that you must have at least one child vomit in the car while on a family vacation. On the fun side, we saw Mount Rushmore, swam at Evans Plunge spring-fed pool, and took an 1880 train ride through the Black Hills. All in all, we had an exciting trip and learned a lot about family vacationing. There are key steps to make a frugal family vacation a success. Here are some things we've learned.

Travel or Home

Decide what is a "vacation" and who is taking it. This one step could save you a ton of money. Instead of planning an elaborate vacation, perhaps staying at home for some downtime is what is needed. If Dad wants time away from the office, then relaxing at home or puttering in the garage may provide a needed break. If Mom needs a vacation, a weekend with girlfriends or guilt-free time doing hobbies may be the ticket for refreshment. These types of vacations cost little, if anything, and can be just as rejuvenating as a tour of France.

Brainstorm Bonanza

Set up a family meeting and brainstorm vacation ideas from all members. This will give the kids a chance to participate and share ownership of the idea. Write down all the ideas, no matter how far-fetched.

Assign Fun Factors

Narrow down the field of choices. This is the perfect opportunity to teach your children budgeting as well as time constraints. To get the most satisfaction for your time and money, evaluate each option according to cost and level of fun. Assign a fun rating on a scale of 1–10. Going on a five-mile hike might rank well for low cost and high enjoyment for the kids. But if Mom is seven months pregnant, an alternative should be considered. Toss out the unrealistic and decide on a destination. Mom and Dad make the final decision.

Day Trips

Your vacation doesn't have to take you far. Day trips are often the best and most cost effective. Explore your own city and state first. You may be surprised at the wealth of entertainment, recreation, and education near your home. How about visiting a working farm, or hitting all the state parks? Contact your local visitor and convention bureau. They will send you free brochures, and many contain coupons.

Activities for All

When we went to South Dakota, we planned a variety of activities that would satisfy everyone's interests. We all agreed we wanted to see Mount Rushmore. It was free and provided interesting lessons on history, construction, and geology. We also got tickets for a vintage steam train ride that we thought was sure to please our boys. But Adam, the avid train lover, fell asleep halfway through the ride. Some events are more satisfying in relation to cost when the kids are older.

Research and Plan

Find out all you can about your destination. Make phone calls, check the internet, peruse a travel bookstore and the library, touch base with a travel agent for free information, and ask others who have been there. Most states and major cities have 1-800 numbers for their travel and tourism departments and send out free material upon request. To find their number, call the toll-free directory at 1-800-555-1212. Many major attractions have toll-free numbers as well. Call and ask if they have reduced rate times or special offers available.

Hotel/Motel Savings

Hotel bills can drain your vacation fund surprisingly fast. Contact the budget-priced motels for a free copy of their location guide. Sometimes you can find quaint motels off the beaten path for a reasonable price. Swing in to the visitor center or ask a local resident when you stop for gas.

To receive a discount, ask for a "blocked" room. These are rooms that need minor repair and are blocked from being rented for the night. However, the room repairs are usually minor, such as a loose towel rack. Some motels will rent these rooms for half price.

Some hotels give discounts to members of organizations like AAA, USAA, or AARP. Ask if these are available.

To stay free, work part-time at your local national chain hotel. Many companies give their employees free rooms anywhere in the country.

Camping

Camping is usually a thrifty option, but make sure you add up all the costs. A campsite price may not include a required state permit, which could significantly raise the actual cost of camping. When we went to South Dakota, we stayed at a state park for $6 a night. This was exceptionally cost effective, until we got rained out. Then we were at the mercy of the tourist season motel prices. We decided that we would save camping for trips closer to home and use dryer accommodations when out of state. Many campsites do offer screened-in shelters, which are rustic, yet fully enclosed.

Other Accommodations

Start your holiday without the Holiday Inn. Other economical accommodations can be found through college dormitories, youth hostels, bed and breakfast homes, and house swap programs. For more information on these, we recommend *Educational Travel on a Shoestring* by Morgan and Allee (Harold Shaw Publishers). Also contact organizations you belong to like homeschool associations, sororities and fraternities, and college alumni groups. Some of these groups print sections in their newsletter or on their websites listing people who are willing to host travelers.

Friend-ly Boarding and Tours

My favorite vacation is visiting friends or relatives. You can visit with your friend in the evening and sightsee during the day when he or she is at work. If your relatives can take a day off, let them be your tour guide. The best way to visit a city is with local residents. They know what's worth seeing and can avoid the tourist traps. When I lived in San Antonio, I had a self-made tour package ready for visiting friends. We could tour that magnificent city all day for under $6 a person.

RV Alternative

If you have a large family or plan on needing several nights lodging during your trip, a recreational vehicle (RV) may be an option. OK, math is involved here. Add up the cost of airline tickets, renting a car, meals out, and overnight accommodations. Then compare it to the cost of renting or borrowing an RV to decide the best alternative for you.

Frugal Advantage

To save your van floors, get a roll of clear floor runner plastic at any discount or home improvement store for about $10. Cut it to fit the floor of your van. To save the seats, lay a beach towel over them. They are easily washed and will protect your seats during family on-the-road picnics.

Batteries

If you need batteries for vacation electronics, our frugal source for AA batteries are photo labs that process disposable cameras. They either throw out the batteries or bag them up to sell. We buy ten batteries for $1 at our local Wal-Mart. They've all been tested and work. Newsletter subscriber Lisa Schwenn of San Antonio, Texas, said she used this tip and had even better results. When she asked the clerk if they sell the batteries out of the disposable cameras, the clerk said she could just have them. Lisa went home with a purse full of free batteries.

National Parks

U.S. national parks are true jewels. Our family went to Yellowstone National Park last year, and it was phenomenal. The geysers and wildlife were awe inspiring. But the greatest surprise was how reasonable it was to vacation there. Once we paid the park entrance fee, there were miles of trails and many natural attractions all for free.

National parks usually offer a variety of overnight choices. Surprisingly, the park's lodging was less expensive than hotels in the neighboring cities. We booked our reservations well ahead of our arrival through www.amfac.com, which administers the lodging, food service, and events in several national parks.

Volunteer Vacation

A wonderful way to learn about different areas of our vast land is to volunteer. My brother-in-law volunteers each summer at a different national park. He enjoys meeting travelers and exploring the park.

You can also find seasonal employment at a national park. When we were in Yellowstone, we met a gift shop clerk who was from Maine. She said she worked at Yellowstone during the summer so she could afford the "vacation." She stayed in the employee dormitory and investigated a new part of the park each day. Tom and I want to do this when he retires.

Traveling with a church mission team is also an excellent opportunity to see the world. You will be doing something you believe in as well as getting to know a new culture, whether at home or abroad.

Off-Season Savings

Vacationing during the off-season will get you the best price for lodging and attractions. The trade-off is some activities are only open during the tourist season. Additionally, some of the flavor of the trip, like street vendors, entertainers, native animal activity, and trees or flowers in bloom may be limited. However, for self-contained destinations like Disney World, off-season is ideal. The lines will be shorter or nonexistent. Find out what attractions, shows, and rides are still open before you buy your tickets.

Packed Park

To make the most of crowded theme parks, get a map beforehand and plan your day. Start your visit from the back of the park and work forward. Eat your lunch earlier or later than the noon hour. This will leave you free to ride the attractions while the crowd is having lunch. Always have a designated meeting place and time in case someone gets separated from the group. Teach younger kids to go to a name-tagged employee right away if they get lost. And wear matching brightly colored T-shirts. You will be able to spot your kids quickly by the dot of bright color in a sea of people.

Working Opportunity

If you or your spouse travel for business, take advantage of the opportunity for side trips. When I was single, I always took a few extra days at the end of a business trip to sightsee in that city. Since my company paid my airline tickets, the only cost for my mini-vacation was a couple nights of lodging. A homeschool family we know travels extensively with the father when he is sent on long business trips. They have spent weeks in Hawaii, France, Germany, Canada, and Australia. What an education!

Meal Money

During vacations we pack our breakfast and lunch, and dine out for dinner. If there is a kitchen available in our room, we make all our meals. When you do eat out, make the most of your dining dollars by experiencing the regional cuisine. Eat fresh seafood at the coast, Mexican food in the Southwest, and don't leave Texas without trying authentic barbecue!

Savable Souvenirs

Souvenirs don't have to cost money. Free collectibles like seashells, bumper stickers, or matchbooks are a good option. Deana's family collected seashell souvenirs from their beach vacation. She put them in a Mason jar, tied raffia around the top, and attached a tag that said the location and date collected.

You can also get souvenirs before you go on your trip. The month before we went to Sea World, I found two stuffed Shamus (Sea World's star killer whale) at a garage sale for 75¢. At the end of our vacation day, I presented the boys with their souvenirs. They were so excited. Just out of curiosity, I priced them at the gift shop and they ran $12.99 each.

If you're buying a souvenir from your vacation spot, get something useful such as a T-shirt, potholder, or dishtowel. You won't have to dust it or store it, and every time you use it, you will have pleasant memories of your vacation. Rather than getting these mementos at a tourist trap, shop a discount store like Kmart or a dollar store.

If you are limited to souvenir shops, they have specials too. When we went to Yellowstone, I asked the gift shop clerk, "What's your best T-shirt for the money?" She showed me an unmarked clearance rack where we got two T-shirts for $5.

Car Trip Games

"Are we there yet?" Ah yes, the plaintive whine of bored children on a long car trip. What's a mother to do? Here are a few suggestions to relieve boredom that won't cost you a penny.

Pack a car activity bag filled with their favorite toys and games. Avoid noisy toys and games with small, easily lost parts.

Check books out from the library about your destination or places along the way. Have a child play tour guide for the rest of the family. Also have kids make their own journal of the trip. To reduce the noise level, ask the kids to write down their messages and "mail" them to each other. If they are too young to write, have them draw pictures of memorable sites.

Audiotapes are great. Check out books-on-tape from your library. Our family loves *Adventures in Odyssey* tapes through Focus on the Family. We borrow several of these cassettes from friends or our church library for long car trips.

Speed Limit Add-Up is a fun and educational game. You add the numbers on the speed limit signs as you spot them. The first one to 500 picks the next game.

Try the fill-in-the-blank game. The first person starts with the letter A and fills in a blank like, "My name is _____ and we live in _____." Keep going until you get to Z.

Play another alphabet game by locating consecutive letters of the alphabet on signs or billboards. (No fair holding the Ritz cracker box outside the window to declare you've found Z!)

Whatever game you choose, remember getting there can be half the fun!

Frugal Flyer

If you fly to your destination, offer to be "bumped" if the plane is overbooked. Deana and her family received free trip vouchers for volunteering to take a later flight. Their vouchers paid for their next family flights. As soon as you check in at the gate, ask if the flight is full. If so, offer to be bumped if needed. The rewards are worth the slight inconvenience if your travel plans are flexible.

Have Fun

Remember the purpose of your family vacation is to be together, learn something new, and come home with wonderful memories. Don't forget your camera—and snakebite kit if you're heading our way!

❧

"When you look like your passport photo, it's time to go home."
—*Erma Bombeck*

Party Like It's $19.99: Frugal Entertaining

Y ou smile and give a gentle wave as you wish your last guest a good night. As you turn from the front door, you view the remains of a perfect party—delicious food, beautiful decorations, and festive music. Another smile brightens your face as you remember that the only thing better than the party was the price.

Is this a dream? Can you really have a great party at a reasonable price? Yes, there is such a thing as elegant frugal entertaining. The above scenario may seem an impossible dream to many, but with a little frugal creativity it can be a reality. Here are some ideas to make your dream party come true.

Invitations

Postcards cost less to mail than regular envelopes. Make your own postcard invitations by cutting off the fronts of old greeting cards and printing the party details on the back. Mail them like regular postcards. If you are computer savvy, print your own invitations or email them free from a website like www.evite.com. For a family party, have the kids make the invitations. If you're delivering invitations, wrap them in small boxes or similar containers.

Limit the List

Keep your party manageable by cutting down the invitation list and setting limits. If the thought of a full-blown dinner party scares you, have a dessert party or hors d'oeuvres before an event. Or host a party with a friend. You'll have half the costs and half the work, but 100 percent of the fun.

Party Themes

When decorating for a party, pick a color scheme and a theme based on what you already have. Red and green are obvious choices for Christmas but if you have lots of blue plates and napkins left over from July 4th, make your party a blue and silver winter wonderland. Throw in some hand-cut snowflakes and you're set.

Borrowed or Bestowed

Make party decorations from what you have first, but if you need other things, borrow them or seek donations. For my (Deana's) daughter Katie's birthday, we decided on a '50s theme. I used pink paper goods we already had and made black construction paper records to hang above the table. We borrowed a '50s music collection CD from a friend.

For a movie star party, I made invitations look like tickets. I decorated with old movie posters donated by the video store, served homemade popcorn in buckets the theater gave me, and played a game with sunglasses from our junk drawer.

Party Favors

As parties have become more elaborate and competitive, so have the party favors. But party favors were meant to be an inexpensive token to help the guests remember the party. For Katie's '50s party, we made snack bowls out of long play (LP) vinyl records. I found the records in my attic, but you can get them at garage sales. To make the bowls, turn the oven on its lowest setting. Place the record in the oven on a sheet of aluminum foil. In one minute, the record will become pliable and warped. Take the warm record out of the oven and push it into a large bowl. This will give it a fluted bowl shape. The record will quickly cool and harden. The girls at the party enjoyed making their party favors and happily ate popcorn out of their own record snack bowls that evening.

Talk Time

A successful party will allow the guests time to mingle and talk to each other. You don't need to fill every moment with expensive food and drinks. Conversation is free. A relaxing atmosphere and comfortable seating is all that's needed.

Music

Set the mood with music. Borrow a library CD of tunes to match your party theme. If you need live music, ask student musicians to play for your party. We have a friend whose daughter is an accomplished harpist. She can perform for much less than an adult professional would charge. If you don't know any musicians, call the local high school, your church, or amateur performing group. They can provide instrumental or vocal performances for less. And they will appreciate the opportunity to perform.

Game Night

Angie had a party for twenty adults at her house recently. The entertainment included multiplayer card games and team board games. She threw in a ping pong tournament in her garage for good measure. She already owned the games, having bought them at garage sales, so the entertainment was free. She even had prizes from her gift box (see chapter 12). It was good free fun.

Make It and Take It

If you are having some girlfriends over for a holiday party, make a craft as your party entertainment. You can make an inexpensive, theme-oriented craft like Christmas ornaments or Easter egg candles (see chapter 4). As you invite your guests, ask them to bring some of the craft supplies. The craft will be entertaining and provide a parting gift.

Party with a Purpose

Every Christmas my sister-in-law has a cookie exchange party. Each guest is asked to bring several dozen of their favorite homemade cookies to exchange with others. This is a wonderful get-together and you walk away with enough cookies to last the entire holiday season. Another productive party involves gathering friends to have tea, talk, and do handiwork like quilting, knitting, or embroidery.

Potluck

Trendy lifestyle magazines are raving about the newly hip potluck supper. Trendy or time tested, the potluck supper is one of the best ways to reduce entertaining costs. No need to be a kitchen martyr. Ask your guests to bring their favorite dish. Most people love sharing their family recipes. You provide the drinks and utensils.

Hors d'oeuvres

Save money by scheduling your party away from the dinner hour and serving hors d'oeuvres. Caterers recommend 10–12 hors d'oeuvres per person. Select a variety of hot and cold appetizers. If your knowledge of finger foods is limited, look in the library for cookbooks that specialize in frugal party food.

Small Plates

Keep the plates small for your gathering. Large plates will encourage people to fill them up, taking more than needed and increasing waste. Smaller plates are easier to handle, walk with, and find places to set.

Garnish

Complete your party dishes with an inexpensive garnish. Leaves from celery or fresh carrot tops make great garnishes. Lemon, orange, or lime wedges will add a thrifty splash of color.

Frugal Food

If you are going to host a dinner, frugalize your menu. Replace pricey asparagus with less expensive fresh green beans. Scalloped russet potatoes will cost less than a recipe calling for red new potatoes. Take your traditional, economic foods and add a special twist like toasted bread crumbs to dress them up for the party.

Tip Top Table

Table coverings turn an ordinary table into a party presentation. Interesting tablecloths can be found at garage sales or thrift stores. But you may already have something that will work well. Use a colorful scarf as a table runner or sheets as tablecloths. Sheets clean easily and most don't need ironing. Tie the sheet at the corners with ribbon for a decorative touch.

Napkins

Cloth napkins dress up any occasion and they're economical. Unlike paper, they can be used again and again. Fabric napkins can be made from almost any material like the Christmas blouse you stained last year. Get a book from the library about napkin folding to make them more interesting. Create your own napkin rings with cookie cutters.

Candles

Candles make your party more elegant. A collection of votive candles or candlesticks makes a beautiful and frugal centerpiece or buffet table decoration. If you're short of candleholders, hollow out apples, oranges, or mini pumpkins and place votive candles inside.

Edible Centerpieces

Create a simple centerpiece with a bowl of red apples or clove-studded oranges. Loaves of home-baked bread and wheat stalks make a beautiful edible centerpiece. Artfully arrange and decorate the food or dishes you're serving as table decorations.

Decorations from Nature

Don't buy expensive cut flowers for your party centerpiece. Save money by using flowers from your own garden or wildflowers. In the fall, make an arrangement of autumn leaves. At Christmas time, use pine boughs or a bowl of pinecones.

Use the Good China

Life's too short not to use the good dishes. Using dishes instead of paper goods will save money. For my daughter's Valentine's Day tea party, I used mismatched china and silver I bought at garage sales. Each place setting was pretty and unique. If you feel your dishes are too plain, use a paper doily to transform them into an elegant serving piece. Even if you're serving an ordinary beverage like water or tea, put it in an elegant pitcher to set on the table.

Ice

Most folks go out and buy ice for their party, but you don't have to. Make your own ice. The week before the party, put extra ice cube trays in the freezer or empty the trays you have twice a day. Store the accumulated ice in a freezer bag. When the day of the party arrives you will have handy bags of homemade ice.

Details

Assure your guests are comfortable and enjoying themselves by attending to the details before the party. Put out enough coasters and set up extra seating. Make sure the bathrooms are clean, functioning well, and stocked with soap, toilet paper, and tissues.

Keep a Record

Record your entertaining successes and problems in a hostess diary. The diary is a small notebook where you document all the party details. Keeping this record will help you repeat your successes and avoid costly mistakes at your next party.

Whether it's a birthday bash or an elegant dinner party, it is possible to entertain and be frugal. Just remember the following principles: do-it-yourself, use what you have, network with others, and be creative. Stop dreaming and start doing. The perfect party is waiting for you.

"May your house always be too small to hold all your friends."
—Myrtle Reed

Smart Gift
Ideas

Your expectations grow as you hand a perfectly wrapped gift to the birthday girl. The gift cost you more than you had intended to spend, but you know she'll love it. You can't wait for her to open it. After the paper is torn off, she politely says, "Oh, uh, thanks." It's not quite the reaction you had anticipated. Perhaps your friend already has this gift. Or possibly she's lacking proper gratitude skills. Or maybe you've given her a gift that didn't match her "love language."

Much has been written on this topic, but Gary Chapman's book, *Five Love Languages,* says it best. He describes how different personality types prefer different types of "gifts." He divides gifts into the following categories.

Gift of Service: A gift of service is doing something helpful for another person. Making meals for a new mom or mowing an elderly neighbor's yard is a precious gift of love and concern.

Words of Praise: "You're such a good friend," or "I like being around you" may speak deeply to your loved one. Put your feelings into words by making your own cards.

Quality Time: Spending time together might fill your friend's or relative's emotional tank. Pencil in a date to have coffee and a pleasant conversation. Share quality time attending your friend's sporting event or special performance.

Touch: What can be better than a big ol' bear hug? To some people, physical touch is the most meaningful form of love communication. Remember when your husband or wife first held your hand? For many, a soft touch or a hearty squeeze speaks volumes.

Material Things: A little present can be a welcomed surprise for those who enjoy material gifts. If this is your friend's love language, give gifts to honor an accomplishment or remember a special date.

Find out which love language gives your friends and relatives the greatest joy. A gift that's truly cherished is more frugal than spending money on a gift that's undesired. Here are some ideas to make your gift giving a pleasure and save money too.

Off the Wall Gift Wrap

Gift wrap shouldn't cost as much as the gift. In fact, it doesn't have to cost anything. Use sheets of wallpaper from discontinued sample books for gift wrapping. You can get these free from home improvement stores.

The Gift Box

The use of this one technique saves our families hundreds of dollars every year. It will do the same for yours! I (Deana) keep a box in my closet labeled "Gift Box." When I run across a super clearance sale or a new item at a garage sale, I buy it and put it in my Gift Box. As a gift-giving occasion comes around, I go to my gift box first and see what's available. Throughout the year as I've gone to sales I've kept in mind the events for which I usually need gifts. I also buy gifts for birthday parties my children will attend during the year. And I look for all-occasion items that are ideal for teacher gifts or acquaintance gifts.

You can also use gifts you've received. If the gift just didn't work out for you, save it and give it to someone else next year. Label it with the gift giver's name so you don't accidentally give it back to them. With the gift box technique, I'm rarely forced to purchase a gift at full retail price.

Package Prices

Weigh your gift package at home if possible, and then call different parcel services to compare prices before mailing.

Gift Planner

For organized gift giving, designate a notebook as your gift planner. Organize it by event, person, or date. I arrange mine by months, one month per page. I write down the person's name along with a specific date, like a birthday. I then jot down gift ideas when they come to mind. For example, I was at a friend's house for a potluck dinner. I saw how frustrated she was at not having enough pot holders. When I got home, I immediately wrote down "pot holders" under her name on the December page. Writing down these ideas keeps me mindful of supplies I'll need if I'm making the gift. I will write these supplies on my garage sale list.

Frugal Gift Wrap

Wrapping paper and bows can be found for just pennies at garage sales. Also save the wrapping paper from gifts you receive to be used again. Strips of wrapping paper can be curled with the edge of a pair of scissors to make a gift topper. Store the paper rolled up to avoid wrinkles; however, wrinkled paper and ribbons can be ironed out with low heat. Iron the inside of the wrap to avoid transferring the paper's ink to the iron.

Solid Gold

Buy solid colored wrapping paper at after-Christmas sales. Solid colors like green, red, and gold are more versatile and can be used for other celebrations throughout the year.

Gift Bags

Bags for presents can be sewn out of fabric scraps or made from brown paper sacks. Shopping bags can be used for gifts by covering the store logo with stickers, or drawings. And a free gift bag is available in some cracker boxes. Just pull out the shiny silver mylar sleeve after you've finished the crackers. Wipe it out and use it for your gift. Fill gift bags with recycled tissue paper, shredded wrapping paper, or Easter grass.

Super Stuffing

If you're sending a package to a frugal friend, use functional packing materials such as dish towels, diapers, sponges, or sandwich bags. The fellow frugalite will put the creative packing material to good use, and your gift will be doubly appreciated.

Alternative Wrappings

Try wrapping a gift in a bandana or scarf. Your child's drawings from school will work too. Some people can scrounge large sheets of paper from work such as architectural drawings, blueprints, or maps. Newspaper and the comics are reliable standbys. Or cut open a potato chip bag, wipe clean and use the silvery inside as your wrapping.

Pinecone Fire Starters

A fire starter is a wax-dipped pinecone that's added to kindling to help a fire start quickly. To make a gift basket of fire starters, collect pinecones from your yard or along the roadside. Put candle stubs or wilted candles in a coffee can or an old cooking pot. Melt the wax on low, adding pieces of crayon for color. Remove from heat and roll the pinecones in the wax to coat them. Arrange them in a basket and attach a gift tag. It's an especially welcomed gift during cold winter months.

Big Is Good

Size makes a difference in a gift's perceived value. For example, if you give a canister set, separate them and put them in a large box, rather than stacked together in a small package. The larger size will look more impressive.

Garden Hose Wreath

A garden hose wreath will bring spring to your loved one's front door year after year. An old garden hose is the foundation of the wreath. Loop the hose into a circle three or four times. Bind the loops together with wire at the top and bottom. Take the remaining hose and wrap it loosely around the circle you've created. Secure this hose with wire as well. Using hot glue, decorate the wreath with empty seed packets, gardening gloves, or a hand spade. Fill it in with silk flowers and dried moss. This makes a great gift for any garden lover. It's also a wonderful way to take things you thought were destined for the trash and give them a new life.

Heavy Is Bad

If you are mailing gifts, be wise with what you select. A heavy gift may cost more than it's worth in postage.

Bed Buddies

Each year Angie and I visit a dear friend at her Victorian home. This year, when we arrived, her warm kitchen was filled with the heavenly smell of cinnamon and nutmeg but her oven was empty. She wasn't baking. She had just microwaved a Bed Buddy.

A Bed Buddy is a scented fabric pouch filled with dry rice or small beans. It can be popped in the microwave or freezer to provide soothing heat or cooling for aching muscles. To make a large Bed Buddy, cut a 12″ x 36″ piece of fabric. Any 100 percent cotton fabric will work, including towels, muslin, old sweatshirts, cut up nightgowns, or flannel shirts. Don't use synthetic fabric or thread as they will melt in the microwave. With right sides together, fold the fabric in half. Sew a tight stitch down three sides of the rectangle. Turn the pouch right side out. Fill with rice or beans. Add potpourri, herbs, spices, or essential oils to the filling. They will release a soothing fragrance when heated. Sew the end shut.

These pads can also be made into trivets, coasters, neck rolls, or shoe warmers. Or keep a mini Bed Buddy in the freezer to take the sting out of little "boo-boos." This is a wonderful gift that anyone can make.

Think Outside the Box

Who says a gift must be in a box? Use what you already have as gift containers: decorative tins, flower pots, glass jars, or decorated oatmeal canisters.

Boot Bird House

Create a home for your feathered friends and a fine frugal gift out of entirely recycled materials. You'll need a child's or woman's boot, a tall tin can, an old license plate, and a wire coat hanger. With a utility knife, cut a 1½" hole in the front of the boot for the birds to come into their new home. Find an empty can about the same diameter as the boot. Slip the can inside the boot, open end down. The can will support the upper part of the boot and keep other birds from flying in through the top. If the can extends above the top of the boot, paint it to match the boot color. Bend the license plate in the middle to create a roof and attach it to the top of the boot. We looped the coat hanger wire through the bootstraps to create a hanger. We made this gift with a boot Angie's son, Adam, had outgrown and their first Texas license plate.

Blue Jean Tote

You probably have a pair of faded blue jeans in your closet right now. With a few stitches, something destined for a garage sale (or the trash) can become a denim purse. To make a purse, cut off the legs and crotch of the jeans. Turn the remaining garment inside out. Sew the bottom of the purse closed with right sides together. You can create handles with the denim fabric left from the legs or use a contrasting fabric such as bandana material. Attach them to the waistband. This makes a fun pool tote. Denim fabric is great for purses because it's durable and thick, but it's also hard on sewing machine needles, so be careful. My thirteen-year-old daughter deemed the purse "cool," so I feel confident this project will win the seal of approval at your house too.

Thrift Basket

Create a gift basket for less. Buy wicker baskets at thrift stores or garage sales for under $1, and fill them with other thrift store finds. I put together a basket of kitchen items, all of which looked brand new, and invested in shrink-wrap to finish it off. The gift looked spectacular for the wedding shower I attended, and it cost me less than $5.

Gifts in a Jar

I saw these cute gifts at a craft show and immediately fell in love with them! A gift mix in a jar is a way of presenting the dry ingredients of a baking recipe in an attractive container. The recipient adds the mix to fresh ingredients and bakes according to the attached recipe. Take a clean quart jar or other glass container and place the dry ingredients of your favorite recipe in layers. Decorate the jar with a touch of calico, ribbon, and a homemade label. Attach the recipe for using the mix. They can be made at the last minute with items you already have on the shelf and with recipes you already know. They also store well, just like mixes from the store. They last up to a year, sealed in an airtight container. Keep in a cool, dry spot. Here's a recipe to get you started:

Nana Ricks' Fresh Apple Cake

Combine in a quart jar:
  2   cups flour
  2   cups sugar
  1   teaspoon salt

1   teaspoon baking soda
1   teaspoon cinnamon
Seal jar and decorate.

Attach the following directions:

In medium bowl, beat together:
1⅓ cups oil
2   eggs
2   teaspoons vanilla

Empty contents of jar into a large bowl and combine with above mixture. Add 3 cups chopped apples and nuts as desired. Mix well. Pour into 9″ x 13″ greased pan. Bake 35–40 minutes at 325°F. Enjoy!

A+ Gifts

Great teachers deserve great gifts. Angie's sons have given their teachers gifts of service. They volunteered to help their teacher clean her room at the end of the year and carry her belongings to the car. But the most appreciated gift, by far, has been the handprint quilt. Angie covers each child's hand with fabric paint and presses it onto a square of material. With the same fabric paint she writes the child's name and the date. She sews the squares together in a basic block design. She uses a blanket purchased at a garage sale as batting and a secondhand, solid-colored sheet for backing. Instead of quilting, Angie draws yarn through the layers and knots it. She hems the edges. Even someone with only basic sewing skills can pull this off and produce an impressive gift. Surf to www.frugalfamilynetwork.com to see a photo.

❧

"There is only one real deprivation . . . and that is not to be able to give one's gifts to those one loves most."
—May Sarton

Happier HolidayS

One Valentine's Day as my (Angie's) husband Tom was putting the boys to bed, Timothy stretched his arms wide and said, "Daddy, I love you this much plus a ga-zillion!" Not to be outdone by his big brother, Adam announced with four-year-old heartfelt sincerity, "Dad, I love you more than a thousand camels." I don't know how to measure a thousand camels, but I do know Adam's heart was bursting with love. Amid all the overpriced red cellophane garb that was available in the stores that Valentine's Day, no *thing* could have meant more than Adam's tender words of love.

On any holiday, just like Adam, express your love and celebration in nonmaterial ways first. Here are some fun and frugal ideas to make your holidays more enjoyable and less expensive.

Make Your Own Valentines

Snatch up after-Christmas clearance sale candy canes and make Valentines! Our brilliantly creative friend Pattie Ferrick came up with this gem of an idea. Take two candy canes still in the wrappers, overlap them slightly, and hot glue them together to form a heart. Candy canes go on clearance sale for 10–20¢ a box. Each candy cane Valentine costs only 2¢. I couldn't buy even the cheap paper Valentine cards for that!

I decorated these with ribbon and they were a big hit at last year's Valentine's party. With a creative eye, you can wisely use the last holiday's clearance items to meet the upcoming holiday needs.

Valentine Sweets

I've always thought making homemade candies was beyond my abilities until I came across this simple recipe for making gorgeous chocolate roses.

1. Mix together 10 ounces melted chocolate chips (1¾ cup) with ⅓ cup Karo corn syrup. Pour onto wax paper. Let stand 24 hours or refrigerate to speed process.

2. Roll the mixture into small, same-sized balls. Press each ball into a petal shape by flattening with your thumb.

3. Starting with a scroll-shaped center, press each petal around it, forming a rose. Add a pipe cleaner stem or one made of craft wire covered with green floral tape. This makes about 10–12 roses.

The next time you eye overpriced chocolate roses in the store window, remember you can enjoy the same novelty at a fraction of the price.

Tuna Cookie Cutter

If you don't have a heart-shaped cookie cutter, make one out of a tuna can. Remove the top and bottom of the can and bend it into a heart shape. This cookie cutter technique became popular in the depression when resourcefulness was at its best.

Freezer Candy

Buy holiday clearance sale candy and store in your freezer. Use this candy to stuff a birthday piñata (see chapter 7), fill Christmas stockings, or bring to school parties. Choose candy that is free of holiday-specific wrappers, like wreaths or snowmen. In our area, candy usually goes on clearance for 50¢ a bag.

"Cheeper" Easter Baskets

You don't have to spend a lot to put together a great basket this Easter. Here's how!

The Basket: Reuse the same basket each year. If you don't have any, hunt garage sales and get a basket that can be used for decorating the rest of the year. And who says you must have a basket? Decorate a gallon ice cream pail or use a pretty recycled gift bag. Remember that large containers cost more to fill.

Easter Grass: Known among us mommies as "Eastro-turf," this plastic grass is inexpensive and will last forever. Reuse any you have for as long as possible. If you don't have any, use colorful tissue paper or pastel fabric scraps.

Edible Goodies: Homemade treats are always the best and least expensive. Individually wrapped Rice Krispy treats, finger JELL-O eggs, hot cross buns, or cookies are great basket treats. To fill plastic eggs for hunting, use candies purchased at clearance prices. Keep in mind that chocolate candy will melt on warm spring days.

Other Treats: Confetti eggs (see chapter 7) are perfect for Easter baskets. Plush toys, fast-food toys, and books about Easter can be purchased at garage sales. Homemade Bible bookmarks and Easter cards reflect the true meaning of the holiday.

Dying Easter Eggs

You can dye eggs (hard boiled, uncooked, or hollowed) with a mixture of one cup boiling water, one teaspoon vinegar, and some food coloring. There's no need to buy the prepackaged dye tablets.

Special Day Pancakes

To honor your loved one on his or her birthday, make mono-grammed pancakes. Pour pancake batter into a recycled squirt bottle (ketchup, mustard, or water bottle). When the pan is hot, squirt out the batter in letter shapes, spelling the person's name. Squirt the mix in the mirror image of the letter, since the pancakes are cooking in reverse. A spin-off of this is to first drizzle the letter on the pan and let cook for just a few seconds. Then ladle more mix on top of the letter to make a full pancake.

I also make holiday pancakes in the shape of hearts, Easter eggs, and fireworks (a starburst pattern with a long streaming tail). I attempted a manger once, but the boys thought it looked more like a four-legged duck. This is a fun and easy way to make a day special without shelling out extra money.

Cake Cost Cutter

To have a professionally decorated cake for weddings, graduations, or baby showers, use this frugal idea. Bake the cake yourself, then take it to the bakery for them to decorate. It costs about one half the retail price, and you still get a professionally decorated cake.

Pumpkin Giveaway

Many gardening centers give their extra pumpkins away after Halloween. Snag a couple for your Thanksgiving pumpkin pie or for decorating.

Holiday Meals

When we were first married and holiday season rolled around, I purchased specialty food for the occasion. In fact, I often spent our entire monthly food budget feeding just one week's worth of company. Over the years, I became wiser about feeding my family and learned that holiday meals don't have to cook my goose.

The frugal trick in holiday meal planning is to serve economical foods, but jazz them up! Rather than a regular baked potato, make twice baked potatoes. Plain rice becomes rice pilaf with the addition of a few peas and chopped carrots. A green bean casserole made with scratch cream soup (see chapter 2), topped with bread crumbs and minced onion, rather than Durkee onions, is an inexpensive side dish. And a corn soufflé is an elegant alternative to plain kernel corn.

Thank You Notes

To make your Thanksgiving dinner memorable, involve your family and guests. Write meaningful Bible verses about giving thanks on small pieces of paper. Roll them into scrolls and tie each with a ribbon. Ask each person to read his verse aloud, describe what it means to him, and mention what he is thankful for. Or write a short personal note saying why you are thankful for each person, and lay it next to each plate. The food will be gone in a flash, but a note of love will stay with everyone long past the pumpkin pie.

Pineapple Turkey

For a clever edible Thanksgiving centerpiece, place a whole pineapple on its side. The pineapple leaves will act as the turkey's tail feathers. Attach a homemade paper or cloth turkey head at the other end.

Tablecloth Memories

Cover your table with large sheets of white paper and have the kids draw a holiday theme on them. To involve everyone, put a pen next to each place setting and have each person jot down a special thought or remembrance. For a keepsake version of this idea, use a solid, light-colored sheet and fabric pens or permanent markers. (Place a liner or pad underneath to safeguard your table.) Use the tablecloth each year and have your family and guests add a new sentiment. Be sure to sign and date each note.

Reindeer Kitchen Towel

This precious homemade gift is perfect for the person that has everything. Purchase white dishtowels at the discount store. They cost about 65¢ each. Paint the bottom of your child's foot with brown fabric paint then press the foot onto the towel. The footprint will form the head of the reindeer. Then paint your child's hands with green paint and stamp them onto the towel as the antlers. Add eyes and a red nose with thumbprints. If you want to make several of these, then make a pattern of your child's feet and hands and stencil them onto the towel.

Hand-a-monium

Your child's handprint on anything will turn a plain gift into a treasure. Handprint tote bags, T-shirts, and barbecue aprons. For a holiday tote bag, I painted holly in the corners and wrote "We Love Grandma" on the side. Leftover latex house paint will work if you are out of fabric paint. "Big" kids can do this too. For my mom's seventieth birthday, all five of us kids put our handprint on a banner. It was a fun and memorable way to honor her special birthday.

Popular Popcorn

Let popped popcorn sit out for three days prior to stringing it for the tree. It will be firmer and easier to thread.

Dough Ornaments

Homemade ornaments only cost a few cents to make and are a heartwarming gift. My boys are always proud to see their prized creation displayed on Grandma's Christmas tree. Mix 2 cups flour and ½ cup salt. Add water just until the dough is workable. Cut the dough with cookie cutters or flatten into a circle and press the child's handprint in the center. With a toothpick, pierce a spot for yarn or ribbon for hanging. Leave the toothpick in during baking to retain the hole. Bake at 250°F for 2 hours. Then turn over and bake 1 more hour. When cooled, paint with paints you have on hand. Dip into shellac to seal in the color. I used some leftover cabinet varnish. Once dried, add a ribbon and mark the back with the child's name and date.

Under Wraps

To decorate your table, cover it with holiday wrapping paper. Lay a sheet of clear vinyl on top of it. You can reuse the wrapping paper and keep the vinyl for other holidays. Clear vinyl can be purchased in fabric departments at discount stores.

Creative Cards

In lieu of expensive Christmas cards, send a holiday letter. Or have your kids color a page from a coloring book and include that with the note. It's a great way to use up all those coloring books.

If you don't normally include a letter with your Christmas card, send holiday postcards instead. Postcards are less expensive to buy and cheaper to mail. You can make Christmas postcards from the fronts of holiday cards you received last year. Dress them up with fancy edge scissors.

Buying Your Family Christmas Tree

Christmas trees are the most popular symbol of the Yuletide season and millions of dollars are spent each year to find the best tree. Whether you prefer live, cut, or artificial, there is money to be saved in your next Christmas tree purchase.

Live Trees: Live Christmas trees are the most expensive of the three choices. They come either potted or with their roots wrapped in burlap. The benefit of a live tree is that after Christmas, it can be planted in your yard. But this choice only makes sense if you were already planning to buy an evergreen tree for your yard and you live in a climate that is compatible with this type of tree.

Cut Trees: Buy a cut tree at a discount store instead of the corner tree lot. Larger stores get a volume discount and pass the savings on to the consumer. You can get trees at deep discounts or even free on Christmas Eve. The trade-off is that the remaining trees will not be very fresh. But since it only needs to last a day or two, postponing your purchase is a frugal winner. Cut-your-own tree farms are available throughout the country. They can't be beat for freshness but compare prices and beware of "experience enhancers" like hayrides and hot cocoa at outrageous prices. Some lucky folks live near a National Forest and for around $5 can obtain a permit from the U.S. Forest Service to thin evergreens from the forest.

Artificial Trees: An artificial tree bought at an after-Christmas sale is far more economical year after year than any other tree.

Free Trees: Cut a tree from your own property. Decorate an indoor, ornamental tree such as a ficus. When college students leave campus in mid-December, check the curbside trash for discarded trees to rescue.

*Tr*eemendous Charcoal

Cut up Christmas tree boughs and use them for charcoal starter when grilling this summer.

Picture Perfect

For instant Christmas decorations, take down your wall pictures and wrap them in holiday paper and ribbons to resemble packages, then rehang.

Christmas Clearance Sale

After Christmas is probably the biggest retail shopping season for frugalites. Here are the deals to look for and the lemons to avoid.

Great Deals: Seasonal items like holiday kitchenware, cards, decorations, and gift wrap have the deepest discounts. I bought large wreaths for 65¢ each and will decorate them for gifts next Christmas. Toys on clearance are great for birthday parties throughout the year. Holiday fabric for tablecloths and next year's craft projects is a good deal. Prepackaged gift sets like ice cream sundae toppings or barbecue sauce gift packs are a wise purchase as long as they are free from holiday markings. They make great gifts during the year. (See chapter 12 for more gift ideas.)

Sales to Avoid: Don't buy anything that you don't need. Even if it's on sale, if you just don't need another set of lights, don't buy them. And skip items that, though on sale, are still overpriced.

Save a Mint

To use up Christmas peppermints, crush into powder and sprinkle over brownies and chocolate cake before baking or add to coffee or hot chocolate. It will give your treats a luscious gourmet mint flavor.

Contentment Robbers

When my boys were little, a trip to Kmart meant a few minutes to ride the mini merry-go-round in front of the store. Though I never put $1 in the machine for the thirty-second ride, the boys would climb on the horses and pretend to go on a cattle drive. Then came one bleak day on the contentment horizon. My boys had just climbed off the merry-go-round when a mom and her young son came up. She offered to have my boys join her son for a ride. She put in four quarters and the merry-go-round began to turn. Timothy, wide-eyed with discovery, looked at me and exclaimed, "Mom! This thing moves?!" The contentment with their pretend cattle drive ended that day.

As adults, contentment robbers reach us in other ways. At holiday time, catalogs, TV commercials, and store displays inundate us with one united message: buy, buy, buy! Prior to seeing the newfangled multipurpose french fry cutter, apple corer, and cherry seed picker all-in-one gadget, we were content with using a knife. To combat this onslaught, pitch the catalogs, hit the mute button during TV commercials, and go to the stores as little as possible. Bypassing the contentment robbers will save your wallet and your emotional peace as well. Pass on the gadgets, and enjoy your own cattle drive.

"I stopped believing in Santa Claus when I was six.
Mother took me to see him in a department store
and he asked for my autograph."
—*Shirley Temple*

Cheap Dates: Romance without Debt

My (Deana's) grandmother grew up on a cotton farm in Central Texas. As a young eligible lady she was courted by two men. The first gentleman caller gave her chocolates to win her affections. The other young man told her he owned a white mule. My sensible grandmother knew that chocolates were here one day and gone the next, but a mule could plow a field day after day. She married the man with the white mule. As far as I know the mule didn't come to the wedding.

My grandfather didn't hide his practicality or thriftiness. As he did, let your dating reflect who you are. Impress your date with your personality and creativity, not predictable over-spending. You'll be glad you let any future mate know your financial values. Whether you are single and courting or romancing your spouse, try these ideas for dates without debt.

Go on a Picnic

Plan a romantic picnic lunch or dinner. Pack heart-shaped sandwiches or small chocolates. Add a personal touch to your own inexpensive, homemade goodies. If you fill the picnic hamper with expensive food, this will not be a frugal date.

Take a Hike

Nature's beauty can be romantic, and it's free. Take your date on a stroll down a hike-and-bike path or on a vigorous walk on a nature trail. Time your walk to view the sunset. I know a couple who took hiking dates, got engaged on a mountaintop, and married at a state park.

Amateur Sporting Events

When my husband and I were dating, we loved going to a Friday night high school football game. Admission was only $2 each for three hours of high-energy entertainment. If you're not a football fan, try basketball or soccer. If you're not a sports fan, that's OK; watching the people at these events is ample entertainment.

Classy Date

Take free or reduced fee classes with your sweetie through a community college or the parks and recreation department. Learn ballroom dancing, a foreign language, or gourmet cooking. If the course runs over several weeks, you'll be guaranteed a date with your loved one every week.

Free Days

Take advantage of free admission days at art museums, zoos, or botanical gardens. Get dressed up and visit the galleries as new showings open. They customarily offer free refreshments. Put your name on the gallery's mailing list, and they will notify you of new shows and exhibits.

Free Events

Every weekend our newspaper lists free events such as outdoor concerts, plays, parades, festivals, charity walks or runs, and exhibits. If you don't subscribe to the newspaper, read a copy at the library or access the newspaper's website or other local event websites.

Light a Candle

Everything is more romantic by candlelight. Prepare an economical meal for your sweetheart and serve it by candlelight on your best dishes with romantic background music.

Make Your Own Fun

Turn off the TV and play a board game, play charades, put together a challenging puzzle, or play cards. These games reveal a lot about a person's temperament and are a good way to get to know your date.

Cultured Dating

Buy last minute "rush" tickets to the theater, ballet, or symphony. Ten to fifteen minutes before a performance, the tickets will be drastically reduced. If you and your date are willing to be flexible, this is a great way to see big shows without the big price tag.

Picture Perfect

Pop some popcorn on the stove and watch a romantic movie you've borrowed from the library. Or go to a movie matinee; they are less expensive and less crowded. When my husband worked for a large computer company, he got discount tickets to movie theaters and other events through the personnel office. Or pull out the video camera and make your own romantic comedy.

Get Out There

Go bike riding, in-line skating, or bird watching. Play a round of miniature golf. Ask about specials or discounts.

Love Letters

Romance your sweetie the old-fashioned way with love letters and poetry. Despite recent increases, a stamp is still a good buy. If you prefer a high tech twist, email your missives through several e-card websites.

Make Your Date Count

Take your date with you to volunteer at your favorite charity. The charity will benefit from your helping hands and the two of you will be spending time together.

It's Your Day

Create a day in honor of your girlfriend or boyfriend. Declare it on a homemade certificate, fix their favorite meal, wear their favorite color, and listen to their favorite music on the radio.

Starry, Starry Night

Spread out a blanket on a clear night at a park or your own backyard. Watch the sunset, catch fireflies, and then gaze at the stars. Your local university may also have an observatory that offers free tours and star gazing hours.

Eating Out

If you go out to eat on your date, try these ideas to save money. Catch early bird specials, drink water instead of ordering beverages, use a coupon, share one large entree, or save the fancy restaurants for dessert only.

Historic Dating

Take your date back in time with a visit to the state capitol, county courthouse, historical society, history museum, or antiques window-shopping. Public building tours are usually free and history museums occasionally request a donation.

Take a Tour

We have a winery near us that offers free tours and tastings of their products. It's the perfect place for a romantic evening out. You could also take your date on a garden or historic home walking tour.

ROMANTIC GIFTS

Diamond Earrings vs. Car Ramps

Romantic gifts aren't always displayed in a jewelry ad; sometimes they're in the auto parts department in Wal-Mart. Tom found this out on our (Angie's) first Valentine's Day together. He figured this traditional day of love called for an expensive gift, so he put some diamond earrings on layaway. As he walked away from the layaway counter, hesitation grew in his mind. He knew the only jewelry I wore were earrings I had had since the eighth grade and a $1.99 Burger King watch.

When he got home, he spilled the beans about his purchase. He wanted to know if I really desired such a gift. I told him how thoughtful it was to buy something special for our first

Valentine's together. "But in all honesty," I said gently, "I'd rather have a set of car ramps."

Tom laughed, but soon realized I was completely serious. He knew he had married a practical woman but even this request was a surprise. I reasoned that although jewelry was certainly special, I would enjoy and appreciate something useful instead. Tom happily exchanged the expensive earrings for a set of sturdy car ramps. Since they were a bit heavy on the earlobes, we have used them for changing oil and other car repairs for over twelve years. The next time you're buying a gift, consider the receiver. Give something to bless them, rather than whatever the retailers hype.

Candy Card

A low-cost and unique gift I made for my husband, Tom, was a candy card. This gift uses candy bar names to write a humorous or sentimental thought. Start with a large piece of posterboard or cardboard, and write out your message. Wherever a candy name appears in the sentence, tape the actual candy bar in that spot. For example, one line might read, "Thanks for all the Good & Plenty Snickers we've shared." Shop around for the best candy prices and decide how large or small you would like your card to be.

How Do I Love Thee

Let me count the ways in an "I love you" notebook. For Valentine's Day, I took a little notebook and wrote one character trait that I appreciated about Tom on each page. Soon, half the book was filled! The cost of this present was only my time. Among all the store-bought gifts he has received over the years, this humble little notebook is one of his most appreciated treasures.

Reach Out and Touch Someone

For long distance romances or even local ones, put your feelings on an audio or videotape. For a small price, you can give a long lasting and meaningful gift. Paint a memorable word picture that will last in their heart forever. Tom recorded two audiocassettes for me when we were dating. They are priceless to me now!

Flowers

Flowers are a typical gift to give to a loved one, but they can be expensive. Pick a bouquet of wildflowers or cuttings from your garden instead. Or give your sweetheart a plant you grew from a seedling.

Up, Up and Away

Tell them how much you care by secretly going to your honey's work and filling his or her car with colorful balloons. Accumulate balloons from free sources like the bank or give-away events throughout the year. What a surprise when they walk out of work and see their car filled with balloons!

Think Small

Instead of buying predictable expensive presents, make your gifts small, meaningful, and interesting. Create a treasure hunt to find the gift, leaving little notes to lead your loved one along the way. The hunt is an exciting part of the gift.

Give the Gift of Service

Sometimes the best way to say "I love you" is with deeds, not words. Wash your sweetie's car, cut the grass, do the laundry or mending, or cook their favorite meal. Homemade coupons for these services make great gifts.

The Way to a Man's Heart

Make homemade heart-shaped treats for less. Bake heart-shaped muffins by placing a marble or foil ball in the muffin tin between the paper baking cup and the tin. Use a squeeze bottle to make heart-shaped pancakes.

"Treasure your relationships, not your possessions."
—*Anthony J. D'Angelo*

Beauty
on a
Budget

I (Deana) have always known that I don't have the most thrilling hair. It's naturally mousy brown and straight as a board. Yawn. In fact, I've seen better hair on a peach.

Before I began a frugal lifestyle, I tried to make my hair more exciting by as many artificial means as possible. I went to a trendy salon to have my hair cut, colored, and permed. I shelled out nearly $150 a visit. After a year of the I-want-to-look-like-someone-I'm-not syndrome I had spent over $700! It was a real drain on our budget. I decided to swallow my vanity and lower my costs.

I started by switching to a less expensive salon. I didn't need to pay extra for a fancy European-style salon to cut my very American hair. I dropped the perm next. God gave me straight hair, so I decided to make the most of it. I then stopped coloring my hair. Blondes may have more fun, but brunettes have more money. Finally, I tried getting my hair cut at an $8 hair styling chain, but my hair looked like I'd gotten in a fight with a weed whacker. So I went up a step on the hair styling ladder. I now go to a training salon for one of the better shops in town.

I get a quality cut for a fraction of the top salon price. It's the best deal for me, and I feel great about my hair.

I'm the same person with the same hair, so why do I feel differently? I changed my perspective. I realized $700 could buy four months of groceries or pay for a summer vacation. We like big hair here in Texas, but you can't vacation in it.

Just because Angie and I don't spend a mint on beauty products doesn't mean we can't look attractive. There are lots of ways to create beauty on a budget.

Saving Shampoo

Make your shampoo last longer by using only a small amount, about the size of a quarter. Use less for shorter hair. If you accidentally apply too much, use it as body wash as it rinses from your hair. You don't have to lather your hair twice in normal shampooing. Despite what the bottle says, once is enough. When you think you've reached the end of the bottle, add warm water and shake. You'll get several more washings.

Hair Conditioner

To treat your hair to a deep conditioning, apply your regular conditioner to wet clean hair then wrap it in plastic wrap or a shower cap. Heat a towel and cover the plastic wrap. Put another towel around your head to keep in the heat. Leave on 20 to 30 minutes.

No Knots

Here's a great homemade de-tangler for pennies. Mix one part hair conditioner with five parts water. Shake well. Use a recycled spray container from your last bottle of spray-in conditioner.

Gum Out

When I was young, I once went to sleep with gum in my mouth. I woke up with it in my hair. My mother used mayonnaise to rub it out. Removing gum or other sticky stuff from hair is a job for something oily. Peanut butter, petroleum jelly, and cold cream will also work. Applying ice to the gum until it is hard and then picking it out is another popular method. It's less expensive than the oily method but requires more effort and time.

Dead Dryer

Remember to clean the air vents on your blow dryer. A friend tossed out her old dryer because it kept overheating. I grabbed it from the trash and with an old toothbrush cleaned the lint from the vents. It worked like new and lasted several more years.

Cost-Effective Cut

Go to a beauty school to get a good cut at a great price. Since the students are learning the trade, the beauty school will charge less than a regular salon. Occasionally, students will need models (no, you don't have to look like Cindy Crawford) to practice a new product or technique. Let them know you are willing to "model" and you'll get your hair styled for free.

Hair Product Shows

For a special frugal treat you can have your hair styled by a world-class stylist. When a hair product show or convention comes to town, they recruit volunteer models. Angie has taken advantage of this top-of-the-line hair care. She traded a Saturday afternoon for a great cut, color, and style. To find out about hair product shows coming to your area, look in the classified ads or call a local salon.

Cut Hair Yourself

To save money between salon visits, trim your bangs and ends yourself. Or have a friend trim your hair. You can also learn to cut your children's hair. For years, Angie has saved hundreds of dollars by cutting her family's hair. The next time you take your kids to the barber, watch closely and ask questions. Invest in a quality pair of hair shears and go for it! If you need more support, check out a hair cutting book or video from the library.

Good-Bye Department Stores

The secret is out. The same corporations that make the costly department-store cosmetics also make the thrifty brands. For example, L'Oréal is made by the same company that makes Lancôme. Estée Lauder produces both pricey Clinique and budget-minded jane.

Secret Formula

The formulas for most cosmetic products are the same. Lipstick is lipstick is lipstick. With only slight variations, the ingredients in the $16 department store lipstick are the same in the $2 drugstore lipstick. If you're buying lipstick at the department store, you're just paying more for advertising and packaging. If you are prone to allergic reactions, however, certain brands may work better for you. Check the ingredients to be sure.

Service Please

You may think you will be giving up service if you buy your cosmetics at the grocery store. But most grocery stores and drugstores have cosmetic counter workers and generous return policies. Often you can return a product just because the color was wrong on you.

Try It before You Buy It

It's always frugal to get the right products. Test cosmetics before you buy them. Tester products have been shared by many people, so avoid germs by using cotton swabs or cotton balls to apply the makeup. If no samples are available, ask the salesperson to open the cosmetic you want to try. They'll be happy to help you.

Turn Back Time

Many products claim to have antiaging properties. They even have brochures that tout their scientific research and their salespeople wear white lab coats. But no one has discovered the fountain of youth. There are no store products that can make your skin younger or stop the aging process. Don't be fooled into wasting your money.

Wear Sunscreen

The sun's damaging rays are the number one cause for premature aging. Prevent your skin from getting wrinkled before its time by using sunscreen regularly. You can also buy inexpensive moisturizers and foundations that contain sunscreen. Make sure the SPF is 15 or higher. Also wear a hat or use an umbrella while out in the sun for an extended period.

All Natural

It's an enticing claim, but there are very few all-natural cosmetics. Most products contain some preservatives or fragrances. Even if the contents are 100 percent natural, that doesn't mean it's better for your skin or a superior product. Don't pay extra for this hype.

Double Duty

Instead of buying liquid eyeliner, use your mascara. Apply it with a thin brush. If your mascara is too thick, run the brush through a little water before applying. Professional makeup artists often drag a thin damp brush through the eye shadow they're applying to create matching eyeliner. If you run out of cream blush, your lipstick will do in a pinch. Apply it with your fingers. Not only is this frugal, but your blush will coordinate with your lipstick. A brown powdered blush or bronzer can be used as eye shadow. An eyeliner pencil can be used as a brow pencil to fill in the brow line.

The Eyes Have It

There's no need to buy many different shimmering eye shadows for evening wear. Just buy a single compact of white pearlized eyeshadow. Stroke it over your regular eye shadow and every color will become shiny and special.

Baby Your Eyes

Newsletter subscriber Susan Howell of Grapevine, Texas, recommends using no-tear baby shampoo to clean off eye makeup. A $1.59 bottle lasts a year, has never hurt her eyes, and is a lot less expensive than department store products. Another eye makeup remover from the cupboard is petroleum jelly. Apply with your finger and remove with a soft cloth.

At First Blush

It can be difficult to walk into a store and pick the right color blush. If you buy the wrong color, don't abandon it to the back of a bathroom drawer. Salvage your makeup mistake. If your powdered blush is too dark, crush it up in a plastic container and mix in baby powder until you reach the right shade. This is also helpful if your blush seems too oily. If your powder blush is too bright, crush in brown blush or eye shadow.

Foundational

If your foundation is too dark, buy an inexpensive ivory color of the same formula and mix them together. Too light? Use the same trick with a darker color. If your oil-free foundation is drying your skin, mix in a few drops of baby oil. When your bottle seems empty, get a few more applications by adding a couple drops of water to the bottle. Use your fingers instead of a cosmetic sponge to apply liquid or cream foundation. A cosmetic sponge is wasteful because it soaks up the foundation that should be going on your face.

Lip Fix

If you've bought a lipstick that's not the right shade, try mixing it with other colors. Apply the too dark or too bright lipstick and then layer on an opposite color until you reach the right shade.

Making the Most of Mascara

An inexpensive mascara will work as well as (or better than) its costly department store sister if applied well. Apply mascara with a clean brush. If the brush has clumps on it, so will your lashes. Wipe off the brush with a tissue. Put on several coats of mascara, separating the lashes in between coats. There's no need to buy a special tool to separate your lashes, simply use the applicator brush from your last mascara that's been washed and dried. And never pump the brush in the mascara tube. This forces air into the tube and dries out the product.

Wash Your Face

The best way to prevent minor acne is to wash your face. Cosmetics lay on the surface of your skin and, combined with excess oil, can clog your pores. Washing your face with warm water will remove the oil, dirt, and makeup. Don't wash your face with bar soap. It will dry your skin. Choose a mild cleanser instead. It should gently remove dirt and makeup from your skin without leaving you feeling dry or oily. Find the least expensive brand that does the job for you.

Exfoliate

Your face naturally sloughs off dead skin cells, so you shouldn't need an expensive product to do this. However, if you feel you need to help this process along, try a mild cleanser mixed with baking soda or ground oatmeal as a frugal alternative.

Pores

Don't pay good money for toners, refiners, or astringents. They're usually full of alcohol or other harsh ingredients. They do make your skin feel taut but only because they dry out the skin's natural moisture. To open pores for deep cleaning, hang your head over steaming water or use a warm compress.

Moisturize

There's no need to buy a separate moisturizer for your body and one for your face. Just look for an inexpensive moisturizer that hydrates your skin and leaves it feeling soft but not greasy.

Feed Your Skin

Your skin is nourished from the inside. A balanced diet, regular exercise, and drinking plenty of water will give your skin a healthy glow, at no extra cost.

Sensitive Skin

If your skin is prone to allergic reactions or acne, avoid products that contain fragrances or are loaded with oils. Look for the words, "fragrance free" and "oil free" on the label. It's never thrifty to buy products that lead to skin problems.

The Scent of a Woman

Buy your favorite perfume at the grocery, discount, or drugstore. Unlike the mall, these stores don't have to pay their employees commission, so the store can sell the perfumes at a lower price. Try perfume "knock-offs" or "copy cats." They can be a great way to get the scent you want without the high price.

❧

"Taking joy in life is a woman's best cosmetic."
—Rosalind Russell

Money Does Grow on Trees: Tightwad Gardening

Last year, Tom and I (Angie) had city friends come to our country home for a weekend. I handed their young children pails and told them we were going to the garden to get green beans and tomatoes for dinner. As we walked out the back door, their five year old looked up at me curiously and said, "But Miss Angie, we can't fit the green bean cans in here. We need a box." When he saw our garden, he was amazed at how vegetables really grew—and was relieved that the little plants didn't have to bear the weight of metal cans.

Gardens provide real life learning as well as money-saving produce. Tom and I currently have 2,500 square feet of vegetable garden space. We've learned many frugal gardening tricks to save money and reap the benefits of this productive hobby.

Dirt Cheap Compost

You must have healthy soil for your garden to produce well. Composting is nature's way of breaking down organic matter into nutrient-rich soil for your landscaping or gardening needs. It's God's original recycling. Anything once alive can be composted. Leaves, grass clippings, and hedge trimmings compost well.

Vegetable and fruit scraps, coffee grounds, and eggshells also compost easily. Meat scraps, bones, cheese, and salad dressings decompose slowly and should be left out of your compost pile. Dump the preferred scraps in a pile or construct a compost bin. There are three popular types of compost bins.

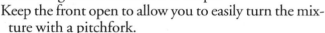

Wire Bin: Deana uses this style with great success in her suburban garden. Bend sheets of woven wire fencing into a circle or a U shape. Keep the front open to allow you to easily turn the mixture with a pitchfork.

Barrel Bin: Use a 55-gallon drum or barrel with a secure lid. Drill several rows of ½″ holes into all sides and set it up on blocks for air circulation. Roll the barrel every few days to mix the contents. Do not use barrels that once contained toxic chemicals.

Three Chamber Bins: Use seven old wooden pallets to make three, side-by-side, U-shaped bins. Stand each pallet on its end, securing them to each other with old wire hangers, nails, or rope. Put compost in the first bin for five days, transfer that pile to the second bin for seven days, and then turn it into the last bin and finally into the garden. I use a version of these bins for our country garden.

The decomposing material and hard-working microbes will naturally heat up. The hotter the pile, the faster it decomposes. Turning the pile will ensure that cold spots on the outside get moved to the hot center.

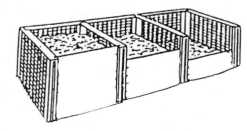

More Dirt Please

If you need more than a bag or two of soil, go directly to dirt companies. They are usually located on the outskirts of town. They are no-frills places where you can buy dirt and other fill material by the pickup load. The cost is pennies on the dollar compared to bags of dirt at a home improvement store.

Frugal Fertilizer

Use free, natural fertilizer from horses, cattle, goats, and sheep manure. It's an excellent addition to your compost pile, or till it into your soil before planting. When we put in our first garden, Tom and I bought bags of manure from the home improvement store. Having grown up on a dairy farm, I couldn't believe we were actually paying for manure. The next year a family with horses moved in down the road. I soon noticed a growing stack of hay and manure outside their barn. I stopped in and asked if I could have their barn cleanings for my garden. They were thrilled to get rid of it and loaded it into our truck with their tractor. As I pulled into our driveway with a pickup full of horse manure, Tom just shook his head and mumbled, "And I used to wax the bed of that truck before we were married."

Natural fertilizer is free and abundant from local farms. If you don't know a rancher, look in your yellow pages for boarding stables. Or call your mounted police division and ask if you can have the manure from their livery. When the circus comes to town, they usually offer elephant droppings to local gardeners. They will be happy to let you haul it away.

Egg-ceptional Gardening

Instead of buying young plants, start seedlings indoors with a recycled egg carton. Poke a few holes in the bottom of each cup for drainage. Tear off the carton lid and put it under the seedling tray to catch water. Fill the cups with starter soil, plant the seeds, and set it on a sunny windowsill.

Deer Repellent

To keep deer from ruining your tree seedlings or garden produce, string empty aluminum cans on a wire near the plants they love. The noise will scare the deer away. A local garden shop had deer repellent spray for $17. My recycled cans did a better job for free.

Hair-Raising Experience

Another deer repellent technique is to surround the edge of your garden with human scent. Get hair trimmings from a barbershop and put them into old pantyhose. Place the nylons around your garden. The scent of human urine will also repel deer. Since I have boys . . . hmm.

High-Tech Gardening

To keep birds out of your garden, use free CDs you get in the mail or old aluminum foil pie tins. Hang them on strings near the plants. The reflection will scare the birds away. Though it looks a bit unusual, we haven't lost a single piece of produce to birds since hanging CDs in our garden.

Growing Tomatoes

Tomatoes are usually the first plant new gardeners grow. Someone once said, "There are only two kinds of people who can't grow tomatoes: the dearly departed and those who've never tried." Picking fresh tomatoes from a vine and not paying for them by the pound saves money. Here are some tips to help you start a crop for your family.

Pick the Right Variety: Pick a breed that's disease resistant and matches your climate zone. People in cooler climates should choose early producing varieties and in warmer areas use drought-tolerant tomatoes.

Start from Seeds: Seeds are cheaper than starter plants but can be tricky to grow. Start seeds indoors in January for the south or March for the north. Set the seedlings on a sunny windowsill. Once they've grown their second set of leaves, transfer them to bigger containers. Recycle large plastic cups, milk cartons, or butter tubs for this job. Just add drainage holes.

Plant the Beauties: Give each plant two to three square feet of garden space in a spot where they will receive six hours of full sun. Since our climate is so hot, we make sure our tomato plants receive morning sun but are shielded by trees in the harshest late afternoon heat. Water the plants deeply in the morning; don't sprinkle. Wait until the soil is dry before watering again.

Support the Plants: Old pantyhose are perfect for tying tomato plants to a stake.

Bug-Be-Gone

Plant garlic, onions, or marigolds around the perimeter of your garden to help keep out pesky bugs. Aromatic herbs like mint, parsley, sage, and rosemary repel insects and should be planted near tender plants. By intermixing these herbs and flowers, you have organic pest control without the high price tag.

Busy Bees

Plant balm, dill, hyssop, and thyme to attract bees. A healthy visitation of bees will increase the pollination of plants and lead to a bountiful harvest.

Vertical Gardening

If you have a patio garden or a small garden plot, go vertical to produce more in your limited space. Lead your plants up a trellis or stake by tying them with old pantyhose. As the plant produces, slip the fruit while still on the vine into a pantyhose sling and tie to the trellis. Deana did this with her cucumbers so their weight wouldn't pull them off the vine. We made fantastic pickles from those cucumbers!

Got Water?

Use plastic milk jugs with holes poked in the bottom or plastic shrubbery pots to drip irrigate plants. Sink the containers halfway down into the soil between the garden plants. Water into the jugs and pots to help stop soil erosion around the base of your plants. This is a cheap way to water your garden plants with all recycled materials.

Have Jug, Will Travel

If you have landscaping that your hose won't reach, recruit a recycled milk jug to help water it. Poke small holes in the bottom of the milk jugs and fill them with water. Carry the jug to the plant and set it down close to the roots. The slow drip action will water your landscape with no need to buy an extra hose.

Holey Hose

If your garden hose is cracked and leaking, don't throw it out. Poke more holes in it and make your own seeper hose. Tom buried our homemade drip hose about 3" down near the plants' roots. Watering is now a breeze as we just turn the spigot on low and let the hose do the rest.

Growing Herbs

Herbs are so expensive in the store. Growing them yourself saves many dollars. And what could be better than stepping outside your kitchen door and clipping fresh herbs for your favorite recipe? Most herbs are wild things and don't require pampering. Herbs do well in moderately rich soil, so don't feed them expensive fertilizers as that may make the plants long and leggy. A more compact plant will yield better flavor, since the oils in the leaves are more concentrated and give off a greater aroma and flavor. Harvest your herbs often. The more you use the plant, the more it will produce.

Demolition Diva

Get free landscaping plants from condemned property. Call a demolition company and ask if you may scour their next job site to find salvageable plants. Older homes may have antique rose bushes, fruit trees, and overgrown shrubbery that can be rescued before they are bulldozed.

Weed Be Gone

Use yesterday's news to weed your garden. Line the dirt between rows of plants with four or five sheets of newspaper. Toss a little soil on top to secure the paper. After harvesting, you can turn the paper into the soil and let it compost.

Tiller Trade-Off

If you can't afford to purchase a tiller, either rent or barter. We agreed to store a city friend's tiller in return for using it once a year. They had less clutter at their small city home, and we didn't have to pay to rent a tiller.

County Extension Office

Free advice, gardening workshops, and how-to pamphlets are available through your county agricultural extension office. They are a wealth of no-cost expert information.

Fishy Fertilizer

When you defrost fish, save the liquid to water your houseplants. It makes ideal fertilizer.

Snake Bait

Erma Drosopoulos, a newsletter subscriber from Venice, Florida, had this creative tip: "My neighbor uses a store-bought snake repellent in her garden. Though it worked, it was quite costly. I read the package and saw the ingredients were basically mothballs and tobacco. Mothballs cost $1 a box and there were plenty of cigarette butts left in the break room at work. I peeled off the paper and crushed the tobacco in with the mothballs. I now have repellent that works the same for a fraction of the cost."

Skate through a Job

Sit on a skateboard while you are weeding a garden bed by the driveway or sidewalk. Instead of crawling along, you glide along your work.

Bottom-Mesh Plants

If you don't have enough stones for drainage when repotting plants, use mesh bags from onions and citrus fruits. Fold them up and place at the bottom of the pot, then cover with potting soil. Mesh bags are also reusable.

Trees for Less

We buy trees in early autumn when prices fall. The home improvement store guarantees the trees for one year. If they don't survive, we take the remains and our receipt back to the store and they provide replacement trees. Also ask the nursery if they have any trees or plants they are throwing away. A drive by their dumpster could reveal plants that aren't sellable but still viable for planting.

Less Lawns

The smaller your lawn, the less it will cost to maintain. Trade a large carpet of green for a smaller lawn with beds of drought-tolerant bushes, ground cover, and flowers. The beds will add color and dimension to your yard and make the lawn more impressive. You'll save on water, use fewer fertilizers and pest controls, and spend less time working on the yard.

Water Efficiently

To test whether your lawn needs watering, take a walk on the grass. If it springs back, you don't need to water. If it stays flat, it's time to water again.

Make the most of your water dollars by watering your garden and lawn in the morning. After 10 A.M. heat steals moisture from watering through evaporation.

A 1″ soaking is needed for deep root growth. Set out an empty tuna can in the area you're watering. When the can is full, the watering is done. According to the American Water Works Association, 85 percent of all landscape problems are directly related to overwatering.

Mow Better

When mowing, cut off no more than ⅓ of the grass blade at a time. Longer grass blades shield one another from the heat and hold moisture longer. If you mow shorter than this, the grass will be "shocked" and turn yellow. Adjust your lawnmower blade to a higher setting to get the best results.

Golf Lawn

Wear golf shoes while mowing to aerate your lawn. The shoe spikes will make hundreds of holes across the lawn, which allow air to come in and break up clay soils.

*"It's difficult to think anything but pleasant thoughts
while eating a home-grown tomato."*
—*Lewis Grizzard*

Save on Suds: Tips for the Laundry Room

We often receive emails from our *Frugal Family Network Newsletter* subscribers asking us about a variety of problems. Here is one we felt had broad application to everyone.

> Dear Frugal Friends,
>   I wash fifteen loads of laundry every week. I have a family of five (two adult children, one high schooler, my husband, and myself). I go through a 100-ounce bottle of Wisk a week not to mention dryer sheets! Any ideas on cutting laundry room costs?
>   —*Barb Pohl, Watertown, Wisconsin*

We can help! Here are some ways to keep your money from going up in soap.

Don't Wash Clean Clothes
Don't wash clothes that aren't dirty. Many times clothes are tossed in the laundry basket rather than put away. Dress clothes that are worn on cool days and don't have a spot or stain won't need to be laundered after each wearing.

Share the Chore

Share the chore with those that create the laundry. Get all household members involved in the laundry task. This will help them appreciate the work involved and make them less likely to toss clean clothes in the laundry basket.

At-Home Clothes

To reduce the volume of laundry at my (Angie's) house, we have one or two sets of at-home clothes to wear. Unless they get dirty or smelly, we use these during the week. This approach has reduced our laundry volume by half and has also helped keep our nicer out-of-the-house clothes in better shape longer. Even fashion-conscious French women do this, so you can too.

Apron

June Cleaver was right! Wearing an apron in the kitchen will protect your clothes from getting dirty. If you're not an apron person, slip on a well-worn T-shirt while cooking or cleaning.

Bath Towels

Reduce the number of bath towels you use. When we were first married, Tom used a new towel each time he took a shower. This habit generated an extra load or two of laundry a week. With gentle persuasion, Tom reduced his towel usage to one a week and was still able to stay fresh and clean. After all, a towel is only absorbing water off a clean body.

Two-Week Towel Cycle

If you share a bathroom with many family members, have each person pick a different color towel for the week. That way each person uses his or her own towel and it's not mistaken for a "dirty" towel. At the end of the week, the drying towel's status is transferred to "floor towel" for the next week. Its new job is to act as a bath mat. At the end of that week, it goes in the wash.

Wash Full Loads

It is more efficient to wash fewer large loads than several small loads. This will save electricity, water, and time.

Soap vs. Detergent

Soap is an original cleaner made from natural ingredients like minerals and fats. It has been used for generations to clean natural fabrics like cotton. Detergents are made from petrochemicals, whiteners, and artificial ingredients and formulated to clean today's synthetic fibers. Though most people use detergents today, you may want to use soap for baby items or if you have skin irritation problems.

Reduce Soap

Reduce the amount of laundry soap or detergent you use. The amount of detergent needed to wash your clothes is primarily a factor of your water's hardness or mineral content. The harder the water, the more detergent is needed. Softer water requires less detergent.

Measuring Cups

Beware of soap measurement cups provided with the laundry detergent. Most fill lines are well below the top. Use a little less than a full cup the next time you wash. Then try a little less and see if your clothes turn out just as clean. Once you've reduced the detergent to the point it's no longer producing clean clothes, bump the amount up a notch. You can probably use about half the recommended amount and still achieve fresh, clean clothes.

Buy Lower Priced Detergents

Less expensive store brands are typically made by national manufacturers. If they don't work out, go back to the best-priced national brand that does the job. Buying a cheap detergent that doesn't clean your clothes is not a bargain. But buying over-hyped, expensive detergent is not necessary.

Price Per Load

Compare "price per load" rather than the weight per box or bottle. Take the price and divide by the number of loads indicated on the box. This will give you a number that you can use to compare between different brands and sizes.

Example:
Brand A $4.57 ÷ 87 loads = .052 per load (5¢ a load)
Brand B $3.95 ÷ 40 loads = .098 per load (10¢ a load)
Brand C $3.50 ÷10 loads = .350 per load (35¢ a load)

Notice the cheapest product, Brand C at $3.50, is the most expensive per load. You may spend less at the checkout stand, but it is not a good value.

Calculator

Many stores will print a per-unit price on the shelf price tag. But they won't do that for marked down detergents in the clearance bin. Take a small calculator with you to figure the price per load. By knowing this number you can be sure you are getting the best value for your money.

Soak Stains

Advertisers try to convince consumers that we need several products for laundry stain removal. But frugal home methods often work just as well and cost less. For particularly dirty clothes, soak them clean instead of adding more soap and tons of washing booster aids. Start the wash cycle and let the drum fill. Add detergent and agitate the clothes for a couple of minutes. Turn off the machine and let the clothes soak for about thirty minutes. Then complete the wash cycle. This is the best technique we've used to help stains release from really dirty clothes.

Stains on Durable Fabrics

For tougher stains on durable fabrics, try the consignment store owner's secret recipe:

Add ½-cup powder dishwasher detergent and ½-cup Clorox 2 to three gallons of hot water. Soak overnight.

Stains on White Fabric

For tough stains on white fabric, scrub baking soda on the stain with a damp toothbrush. If more power is needed, Barkeeper's

Friend scouring powder made into a paste is quite successful at removing stubborn stains.

Spot on Collar

If you get a spot on an inset collar, the solution is simple. Take the collar off and turn it over. With a seam ripper, carefully detach the collar from the shirt. Flip the collar over so the spotted side is facing down. Insert it back into the original seam and reattach. Your shirt will be saved, and no one will know there's a spot hiding under the collar.

Bleach Spot

Accidentally splash some bleach on a shirt? When this happened to Deana, she made a '60s tie-dye shirt from the "ruined" garment. Tightly twist a small section of the shirt and secure with a rubber band. Continue doing this until the entire shirt is in a series of tightly wound wads. Mix a solution of two parts water to one part bleach, place in a squeeze bottle, and squirt the bleach solution on the shirt. Rinse the shirt with the rubber bands still on, but remove them before drying. Enjoy your groovy new shirt.

More Bleach Spots

Another approach to dealing with bleach spots it to cover them up. A workshop attendee showed us her skirt. It was a nice denim fabric with a shower of hearts trickling down the side. She said that under the hearts were tiny bleach spots she covered up with heart-shaped patches.

THREE BASIC STEPS TO STAIN REMOVAL

- Stains are best treated immediately. The quicker you get to them, the more likely you will get rid of them.

- Blot, don't rub, a stain to try to remove it initially. Rubbing may spread or grind in the stain.

- Start with cold water. Heat will set a stain.

Frugal Stain Removal Guide

Stain	Action
Adhesive sticker tape or gum	Put the garment in the freezer to harden the sticky residue. Scrape with a dull knife. If not completely removed, make a paste of laundry detergent and work into the residue. Launder as usual.
Ballpoint pen	Spray with a small amount of hair spray. Work the hair spray into the stain. Rinse under cold water.
Blood	Rinse the stain under cold water. (Hot water will set the stain in the fabric.) Wash in cold water with two to three cups of hydrogen peroxide.
Crayon or wax	Scrape off with a dull knife. Place stain between white paper towels and press with warm iron. The wax will transfer to the towels. Change paper towels frequently so as not to transfer the stain to another part of the garment.
Grease	Generously apply baby powder or cornstarch to stain to absorb grease. Then work in a small amount of shampoo. Launder in the hottest water that is safe for the fabric.

Liquid Softener

Liquid fabric softener is generally less expensive per load than dryer sheets. But if your washer doesn't have an automatic softener dispenser and you want the convenience of a dryer sheet, try this homemade alternative. Dampen an odd sock with liquid fabric softener and toss it in the dryer. People have been making this version of a dryer sheet ever since the electric dryer first came on the market.

Dryer Sheet Alternative

Another dryer sheet alternative is to fill a clean spray bottle with equal amounts of water and liquid fabric softener. Spray the dryer drum with three or four sprays, and then load clothes.

Versatile Vinegar

Out of liquid softener? Use vinegar in its place as it will soften clothes and reduce static cling. Use the same amount of vinegar as you would fabric softener. The clothes will smell vinegary coming out of the washer but not when they emerge from the dryer. It also can be a helpful disinfectant and is ideal for adding to a load of diapers or dishtowels. Do not use vinegar as a rinse though if you used bleach in the wash cycle as it may cause dangerous vapors.

Halve It

If you are loyal to purchased dryer sheets, tear them in half or thirds and reuse them as long as possible. When I was single, I lived in an apartment complex with a community laundry facility. I never bought dryer sheets because there were plenty left in the laundry room. They were used only once, and I found they were perfect for another load.

No Softener Needed

The purpose of a dryer sheet is to prevent static cling and soften clothes. You may not need dryer sheets in the summer or humid weather when static cling isn't a problem. If you have soft water, your clothes may come out of the dryer already softened.

Reduce Drying

Reducing your drying time will save money also. Hang up your dress clothes after just a couple minutes in the dryer rather than a full drying cycle. Less hot drying will also help your clothing last longer since concentrated heat will speed deterioration of the fibers.

Clothesline

The old-fashioned clothesline, now the trendy "solar dryer," can save you about $5 a week in dryer utility costs. That's not counting the electricity used to cool a house overheated by a hot dryer.

Baby-Gate Dryer

Versatility is key to a successful frugal life. Put your baby gate over the bathtub and lay your sweaters on it for drying.

Laundry Basket Repair

For laundry baskets with split weaving, take yarn or thin rope and weave over the rupture. This will prolong the life of your laundry basket.

Spray Starch

I've had moderate success with mixing one or two tablespoons of cornstarch with one cup water, putting it in a spray bottle, and using it as a spray starch. I spray it on the inside of Tom's dress shirt and iron. Shake the bottle prior to spraying to keep the solution from clumping. I only do this when absolutely necessary because most shirts don't need to be starched, in my opinion.

Dry Cleaning I

Dry cleaning can shrink a budget fast. To save on dry cleaning, don't buy things that need to be dry cleaned. That's a no-brainer but one that's frequently overlooked.

Dry Cleaning II

If you do have a dry clean only garment, keep it clean by wearing a tight T-shirt underneath to absorb perspiration and body odor before it reaches the garment.

Dry Cleaning III

Try freshening your garment by placing it on a hanger in front of an open window. Some garments marked "Dry Clean Only," such as sweaters and rayon blouses, can be safely hand washed in Ivory Soap Flakes, not detergents. In general don't hand wash wool, suits, or coats. We've also had good experience with a home dry cleaning kit. They don't actually "dry clean," but they do freshen and that's often sufficient.

Dry Cleaning IV

The last resort is to compare prices if a full cleaning is needed. Be sure to look for coupons in the back of your phone directory. Ask if the cleaner will give a discount if you take in a pile of wire hangers for them to recycle.

꒰ꢀ

"I believe you should live each day as if it is your last, which is why I don't have any clean laundry because, come on, who wants to wash clothes on the last day of their life?"
—Mark, age 15

A Winning
Wardrobe: Pocketing
Savings on Clothes

Angie and I (Deana) have had the privilege of speaking to many audiences. For both TV appearances and workshops, we dress in casual office wear. They're the kind of clothes you would wear to an office that doesn't require suits. Our clothes are clean, stylish, and depending on the number of carpools we've driven, wrinkle free. We were wearing just such attire at a recent workshop.

As we began to receive questions, a young lady half jokingly commented, "You two can't really be that frugal if you wear clothes like that." Apparently, this woman thought our clothes were too good to be frugal. I looked down at my clothes because I had forgotten what I was wearing. My quick inventory revealed that everything I had on was passed along to me by my mother. My wool slacks, silk blouse, and leather belt had all come from her. My classic black leather shoes were purchased almost seventeen years ago. Angie was wearing black slacks that she had bought at a thrift store when they offered "fill-a-bag" for $3. She had paired that with a coordinating shirt she bought at a garage sale for 50¢. She also wore a classic jacket that's still going strong twelve years after she bought it.

We are familiar with this woman's misconceptions. The common fallacy says that thrifty people wear clothes that are shabby and outdated. They don't look stylish or fashionable. Not true! We wear sophisticated clothes; we just don't pay sophisticated prices. Here are some ideas to maintain a winning wardrobe for pocket change.

Nothing to Wear

Before you buy even one more thing, decide if you need it. You probably already have a closet full of good clothes. But they may be obscured by poor fashion choices still loitering on the hangers. Pare down your closet. Weed out the dated fad items. Box them up for your next garage sale. Remove duplicates. No one needs five blue T-shirts. Thin your selections. If you're a stay-at-home mom, you probably only need four or five nice dresses for church or special events, not twelve. Make sure the remaining items coordinate with each other.

It's a Classic

Maintain a classic wardrobe. Classics are garments whose style lasts through many years, even decades. Blue jeans, a white blouse, a navy blazer, black pumps, polo shirts, and khaki pants are all timeless. These classics should be the backbone of your wardrobe. In the long term, traditional clothes will cost you less than a fad-of-the-week wardrobe.

Makin' a List

Many people go grocery shopping with a list, but few think of going clothes shopping with a list. A list will prevent you from buying duplicate items or clothes that don't coordinate with your existing wardrobe. Make a list of the few classics that may be missing from your closet, and carry it in your wallet. List sizes, color, and fabric choice. If you're trying to match the color of something you already have, snip a bit of fabric from the seam allowance and tape it to the list.

Cheap or Cheaply Made

When buying classic clothing, select pieces that are well constructed and durable. When you're trying to save money, it's tempting to buy cheap clothes at cheap prices. But poorly made garments won't last. A $5 blouse that falls apart after only two wearings will give you a very high price-per-wearing. It's wiser to get quality clothes at cheap prices (or free) through garage sales, thrift stores, and pass-along networks. A better-constructed blouse purchased at a garage sale for 50¢ and worn for years is a much better buy.

Pass-Along Clothes

Free is always good. If you have someone who is willing to pass along clothes to you, rejoice. My mother has given me many wonderful outfits, and Angie has a network of friends that pass good clothes to her. We, in turn, pass along our gently used clothes to others. This network of friends and relatives is our primary source of clothes. (See chapter 7 for more on passing along clothes.)

Clothes Swap

Get free clothes by hosting a clothing swap with your friends or through a club. Bring all your best clothes to exchange.

Garage Sales

We can't say enough about garage sales. That's why we wrote a whole chapter about it earlier. Garage sales are full of thrifty clothing for kids and adults. If you are a petite woman and wear a size 8 or smaller, run, don't walk to the nearest garage sale. Garage sales are teeming with smaller size clothes because, frankly, the rest of us grew out of that size a long time ago. Since there won't be a dressing room available at a garage sale, wear bike shorts and a snug T-shirt. You can slip garage sale clothes on over them.

Thrift Stores

If you can't completely develop your wardrobe through pass-along and garage sale clothes, try the thrift store. Thrift stores cost more than garage sales but they are almost always less than the mall. Be aware of prices for similar garments at various stores, so you don't pay more for something at a thrift shop that is available new at a discount store.

If a particular brand is important to you (or your teen), the thrift store has them. You will actually find a wider selection of labels at the thrift store than you could at any single department store. Some folks are concerned about the sturdiness of a second-hand garment. But if a piece of clothing has lasted long enough to make it to the thrift store, chances are it's pretty rugged. Thrift stores also have discount days and coupons. Ask the staff about senior, military, or student discounts. And ask when new merchandise is put out. If you arrive on that day, you'll get the first look at the new selection and have first crack at clothes being marked down to make room for the new arrivals. Be patient. It may take several trips to find what you're looking for.

Resale or Consignment Store

Resale shops sell used clothing at prices just below retail. The selection at these stores can be better than the thrift store, which must rely on donations. Resale stores get their inventory from individuals looking to sell their gently used clothes. The storeowner picks only the best items to sell. If you desire a voguish look, try consignment stores that deal only in vintage or retro clothing.

Season Less

Fill your wardrobe with garments that are versatile, all-weather clothes. A raincoat with a lining that zips out can serve the purpose of two coats. It can be worn more months out of the year because it's both lightweight and insulated.

Cheap Frill

Choose clothes that have little or no ornamentation. Frilly lace, sequins, and beads that are used to decorate clothes come off easily and show wear quickly. They often require the added expense of dry cleaning. And they look outdated sooner than unadorned clothes.

Checkin' It Twice

Whenever you buy clothes at a garage sale, thrift store, or resale shop, check the item for defects. Look for stains, rips, worn-out fabric, or seams. Make sure all zippers and clasps work properly.

Repair Don't Replace

Mend your clothes; it's cheaper than buying new ones. Repair trim, lace, elastic, zippers, clasps, and buttons to make your clothes like new again.

Button Up

Newsletter subscriber Jackie Garner of Friendswood, Texas, says she's learned a trick for sewing on buttons. With a four-hole button, sew only through two holes and tie off. Repeat this for the other two holes. If one thread unravels you won't lose your button. Adding a drop of clear fingernail polish will also keep the threads from unraveling too quickly.

Pantyhose Repair 101

When pantyhose get small pulls in them, don't throw them out. Try dotting the spot with clear nail polish both inside and out and then clipping off the pulled strand. Or wear your hose inside out; the pulls will be less noticeable.

Saving a Sole

If your favorite pair of sandals has a side strap that keeps coming out of the sole, try hot gluing it. Squirt hot glue down into the empty pocket that holds the strap. Insert the strap and press down firmly. Be careful when working with hot glue! It can burn. Clamp the assembly together with clothespins and let cool. This technique has stretched the life of several pairs of shoes in our families.

Standing Tall

Keep knee-high boots standing tall by putting rolled up magazines inside. The magazines will provide support and keep them from flopping over at the ankle.

Lost Soles

Check with the local shoe repair shop for good deals on shoes that have been abandoned. If customers bring in shoes to be repaired but never return to claim them, the shop will sell them at reduced prices.

Fresh Feet

Eliminate odor in your shoes by sprinkling baking soda in them instead of a pricey foot powder. Or fill old knee-high hose with fresh, absorbent kitty litter and place into the shoes to devour smells.

From Ear to There

If you lose an earring, don't throw the mate out, wear it on your collar as a decorative pin. Or sell the loner at a garage sale—a perfect find for guys who have one ear pierced.

Teddy Bear Jeweler

Use a teddy bear to store your jewelry. Loop necklaces around his neck and bracelets on his arms and legs. Attach pierced earrings to his ears. You'll have the best dressed bear in town and free jewelry storage.

Best Dressed

Use material from old bridesmaid dresses to make scented sachets for your lingerie drawers.

Iron Cleaning

To clean an iron and avoid making brown spots on your clothes, mix ½ cup vinegar and ½ cup water. Pour it in the iron and set it on "steam." Hold the iron horizontally and let it steam until all the water evaporates. Repeat with 1 cup water. Wipe clean.

ào

"I base my fashion taste on what doesn't itch."
—Gilda Radner

Clean Up on Savings: Economical Cleaning

Most people have a different cleaner under the sink for every surface in their house. You might be surprised to learn how few things you need to clean your house—and those have been sitting on the shelf all along. The Frugal Friends' Laboratory (Deana's house) was the site of an intense consumer investigation. We pitted several national-brand cleaning products against frugal homemade cleaning recipes and let the products duke it out. Here are the results of our comparison:

Window/Glass Cleaners

In this category, there were two homemade recipes that worked well:

Recipe A: 1 tablespoon ammonia and 1 cup water (less than 1¢ per ounce)

Recipe B: 1 cup vinegar and 2 cups water (less than 1¢ per ounce)

Recipe A was the best performing. It cleaned well and left no streaks. Recipe B cleaned fairly well but left a vinegar smell.

Compared to Windex at 7.8¢ per ounce and store-brand cleaners, which cost 4.6¢ per ounce, both homemade recipes were big money savers. Only one store-bought alternative, windshield wiper fluid, can compete in price. A gallon of wiper fluid for $1 is less than a penny an ounce.

Toilet Bowl Cleaners

The battle of the bowl came down to two good recipes:

Recipe A: 2 tablespoons bleach (less than 1¢ per ounce)

Recipe B: 1 tablespoon vinegar and a "sprinkling" (1 tablespoon) of baking soda (1.3¢ per ounce)

Both cleaned well and cost about the same. When added above the water line, vinegar and baking soda produce a fizzing action that might get some junior scientists interested in cleaning the bathroom. However, the bleach solution is more convenient, disinfects, and leaves no grit. Both of these recipes beat the prices of national brands, which run about 6¢ per ounce.

Floor Cleaners

To clean vinyl and other nonporous floors, two simple recipes will do the trick:

Recipe A: ¾ cup bleach and 1 gallon water (less than 1¢ per ounce)

Recipe B: ½ cup ammonia and 1 gallon water (less than 1¢ per ounce)

Each recipe worked well. Both cleaners are less expensive than national brands that cost 5–8¢ per ounce.

Furniture Polish

I (Deana) don't know if many people actually "polish" their furniture anymore. I simply dust with a damp rag, but if you have an antique dining table or an heirloom china hutch, polishing may be in order.

The Frugal Friends' Lab found only one homemade recipe for polish. Combine the juice of 1 lemon, 1 teaspoon olive oil, and 1 teaspoon water. Apply it to the surface, let it stand for 5 minutes, and then buff to a shine. This homemade polish costs 23.7¢ per ounce. It worked as well as Pledge, which costs 26.2¢ per ounce. However it required more time and elbow grease. It also couldn't be stored on the shelf, so you must make it fresh each time. On the positive side, if you didn't like the results, you could always put this concoction on your salad. In the final analysis, a national-brand polish, such as Kleen Guard, which costs 11.9¢ per ounce, is fine if you must polish. We suggest you use it sparingly.

$$- \pmb{\$} -$$

As you can see, bleach, vinegar, and ammonia are effective cleaners. They are the main cleaning supplies used by our friend who runs a house-cleaning service. We don't need all the fancy cleaners on the grocery store shelves. In fact, most national-brand cleaners are just versions of the recipes listed here. By using these few ingredients, you can save money and help the environment by purchasing and throwing away less.

Cleaning Safety

For safety and convenience clearly mark containers of home-made cleaners. Label them with the recipe and what it cleans. Add food coloring to help you identify them on sight. *Never mix ammonia and bleach or products that contain bleach.* The combination can produce toxic fumes. Remember to use common sense when working with any household cleanser. Precautions such as rubber gloves and good ventilation are always smart and frugal.

Little by Little

Don't let cleaning overwhelm you. Clean a little each day and have family members help. De-clutter before you start cleaning. There's no need to clean stuff you will eventually throw out. Clean only what's dirty and don't go over what you've already done. If you only have a few minutes, break the task down to a manageable size. Clean just one room or part of a room instead of trying to tackle the whole house.

Top to Bottom

Start at the top and work your way down when cleaning a room. This way dirt will not fall on something that's already cleaned, like the floor. Working from left to right will help you keep track of what's been cleaned and prevent backtracking.

Take It with You

Put all your cleaning supplies in a bucket to carry from room to room. Or tote them in a carpenter's apron with large pockets. If you have all of your supplies handy, you won't need to run back and forth getting them, which wastes time and energy.

Rags to Riches

I can't think of any reason to buy a cleaning cloth. I have plenty of soft cloths for cleaning and they're all free. My box of cleaning cloths includes odd socks, old underwear, stained T-shirts, and tattered towels. Cleaning rags can be washed and used again. Even if I toss one out because it's become too filthy, I can depend on my family to make a new one to take its place.

Old News

Use old newspapers to clean your windows instead of paper towels. I've done this for years and the ink has never come off on the windows. Newspapers don't leave lint like paper towels and they're cheaper.

Do-It-Yourself Duster

The disposable dusting mops advertised on TV are popular. Did you realize you can make your own at home? Take a small swivel dust mop and tape on a used dryer sheet. Throw away the sheets when you're done, just like the commercial. It costs nothing to reuse the dryer sheet you were going to throw out anyway.

Rock around the Mop

Fill the house with upbeat music you love. It will make cleaning more fun and it'll seem less like a chore. You'll also move faster and be done more quickly.

Webbed Wonders

To get rid of cobwebs in high corners, slip an old T-shirt over the end of a broom and dust them away. This costs nothing, compared to an expensive extension wand duster.

Dapper Drapes

To dust drapes, remove them from the rod and pop them in the dryer. Toss in a damp towel to attract the dust. Fluff on a no-heat setting for ten minutes. Rehang immediately to prevent wrinkling. If you have fabric blinds, spray them with antistatic guard to help repel dirt.

Wall Art

My sister called one day and reported that my nephew Sam had discovered the joys of art. Unfortunately, he had rendered his artistic masterpiece on their living room wall! To remove crayon marks from walls, spray with WD-40 and let it sit for five minutes. Blot with a paper towel and then clean with soap and water. If your junior Picasso is into markers and ink, try spraying the spots with hair spray. Rub with a soft cloth, and then wash with soapy water. Always test in an inconspicuous area first. If all else fails, paint over it or have the artist sign it and frame it.

Screen Clean

When cleaning computer or TV screens, never spray the cleaner directly onto the glass. The cleaner may drip down the screen into the components, which are costly to repair. Instead, spray the cleaner onto a soft cloth, like an old sock, and clean as usual.

Ashes Away

Lightly spritz ashes in the fireplace with water to dampen them before cleaning the hearth. This will reduce the amount of dust that is created when you scoop out the ashes.

Cool Clean Up

Clean refrigerator produce bins with vinegar and water to help prevent mildew. To clean under the refrigerator, secure an old sock to the end of your broom handle with a rubber band.

Don't forget to pull the refrigerator away from the wall and dust the coils. The refrigerator will run more efficiently and use less electricity after a good cleaning.

Shiny Sinks

Removing water spots and stains from your sink can be challenging, so here are a few tips. Clean water spots by rubbing them with vinegar and a soft cloth. Or use baking soda and water. Rinse clean and dry with an absorbent cloth. Tackle stains with a paste of rubbing alcohol and baking soda. For stubborn stains, scrub with a mixture of baking soda and bleach.

Burnt-On Food

To loosen burnt food on cookware, fill the pan with one or two inches of water and simmer for a couple minutes. Then wash as usual. This may salvage pots you thought were hopelessly ruined.

Wash Your Washer

Is your dishwasher looking dingy? Send your empty dishwasher through a regular wash cycle with only ½ cup of liquid bleach. It will brighten the inside to a sparkling clean look.

Clean and Crazy

To thoroughly clean kids' "crazy straws," soak in a solution of 1 tablespoon bleach to 1 quart hot water. Rinse with hot soapy water.

Hard Water Stains

To clean hard water stains in your toilet, shock treat it with straight bleach. If the stain doesn't budge, we suggest using a pumice stone. Empty the water from the bowl, and rub gently with the stone to scrape off the mineral build up. The stone can scratch the porcelain, so be careful. Start scraping in the least noticeable spot first.

Squeegee Clean

Prevent hard water stains and soap scum from building up in your shower. After every shower, use a squeegee to remove water from the shower walls and door. A squeegee that's all rubber, no metal parts, can be left in the shower without fear of rusting. If you don't have a squeegee, a towel works well also.

Mildew

You don't have to buy an expensive mildew cleaner at the grocery store. Use this homemade cleaner instead. Add 1 tablespoon of bleach to a spray bottle and fill it with water. Spritz the bleach solution on your tub, shower tiles, and shower curtain to clean mildew. If you keep the bottle in the bathroom and spray the tile after each shower, mildew won't have a chance to develop. Don't use this mixture if your tile grout is dark, and avoid spraying it on metal fixtures.

Polishing Your Pearls

Newsletter subscriber Katherine Arnone of Portland, Oregon, recommends using toothpaste to polish silver, brass, and some jewelry. She says it works better than the chemical products. It's inexpensive, nontoxic, and you always have it around the house.

Stuck on Stickers

Did junior plaster his headboard with colorful decals? Warm the unwanted sticker with a blow dryer set on medium. The heat will loosen the adhesive and make the sticker easier to remove. If there is any adhesive left, clean it with fingernail polish remover (acetone). Test the effects of acetone on a hidden area first.

Better Baseboards

Clean baseboards without breaking your back by wearing old socks dampened with water. Drag your feet along the baseboards as you clean.

Floor Eraser

To remove dark skid marks on the floor made by rubber-soled shoes, simply rub with an eraser.

≈❧

"Cleaning the house while children are growing, is like shoveling the walk while it's still snowing."
—*Phyllis Diller*

Driving Down Car Costs

I (Deana) have run out of gas only once in my life. I was single, living a thousand miles from my family, and determined to make it on my own. But I was not the world's best money manager and by the end of one particular month, I was flat broke. I was trying desperately to make it to my next paycheck. I needed gas in my car, but the only money I had was the change in the ashtray. The day before my coveted payday, my car was finally overcome by a steady diet of fumes. I called a kind coworker to pick me up from the side of the street. She gave me a ride and bought me a tank of gas. I was thankful, but very embarrassed. I prayed I would never run out of gas or money again. I've since become a better money manager and learned easy ways to save money on car costs.

Plan Your Driving

Cutting down on the number of short car trips is the easiest way to save money. Determine if your trip is necessary before you leave the driveway. Angie is great at this. She lives in the country about twenty minutes from town. She carefully weighs the value of a car trip and plans her errands thoughtfully. She is a master at combining trips—another great way to save and avoid backtracking. According to the U.S. Department of Energy, short trips are wasteful. Travel of five miles or less accounts for only 15 percent of all miles driven, but burns 30 percent of the gasoline.

Idle Time

When running errands, choose a time when traffic is light. This will minimize the stop-and-go routine of congested traffic. When you are forced to wait in traffic for more than a minute, turn off your engine. Restarting your car will take less gas than letting it run. If you're in the habit of waiting in drive-thru lines for more than a minute, park the car and go inside. Remember if the car is off, gas consumption stops.

Drive Smart

How you drive your car can save gas. On the highway, lowering your speed from 70 mph to 55 mph will net you 20 percent more miles per gallon of gas. Drive at a steady pace. Accelerate and decelerate smoothly and avoid stomping on the gas or slamming on the brakes. Jerky driving burns 50 percent more gas than normal driving, according to the U.S. Department of Energy.

Maintain It Yourself

Good auto maintenance will increase your fuel economy and give you a reliable car with fewer repairs. Change your air and fuel filters regularly. Dirty and clogged filters reduce fuel economy. Do regular tune-ups. Without them, your engine can use up to 9 percent more gasoline, say government experts. Save money by doing your own oil changes. Be familiar with the recommended maintenance schedule for your vehicle. Learn how to check or replace the belts, hoses, spark plugs, filters, and fluids.

Thrifty Tires

Buy radial tires as they are the most fuel efficient and last longer. No matter what tires you have, be sure they are properly inflated. Underinflated tires can reduce fuel economy by 2 percent for every pound of air pressure under the recommended inflation. They also wear more quickly, need to be replaced sooner, and are the main cause of blowouts. Make sure your tires are properly aligned. This will save gas and wear on your tires.

Buy a Blemish

If available, buy "blemished" tires. These are tires that have a minor cosmetic imperfection. The structure and safety are not compromised.

Lighten the Load

Remove any excess weight from your vehicle. If you haul sports equipment or tools on the weekends, be sure to take them out before your commute to work on Monday. A lighter car uses less fuel.

Frugal Fuel

Shop around for the best price on gasoline. Pump it yourself and pay cash to get a discount. Cheaper gas prices can often be found at cash-only gas stations or out-of-the-way locations.

Park It

Leave the car in the garage. Walking, biking, or taking the bus are all good ways to save money on gas and reduce vehicle wear. It's also friendlier to the environment.

Carpooling

My neighbor rides to work every day in a vanpool. The vanpool program allows several people to commute to work in a city-sponsored van. Each member of the pool pays only $25 a month for the transportation. If you are willing to fill out monthly records, you can be a van driver and ride for free. The vanpool is convenient, reliable, and a frugal way to get to work. Traditional carpooling among coworkers is also thrifty. You'll save on gas, parking, and frayed commuter nerves.

Parking Penny Pinchers

Parking is often at a premium in urban areas. If you commute downtown for work, these costs can add up. Save money on parking fees by finding a lot or garage farther away from downtown.

The walk will give you a built-in exercise program. If you must park in town, adjust your schedule to arrive early and beat the crowd to any free spots. Or ask residents or businesses if they would rent a parking space to you at a reasonable monthly rate.

Winter Wheels

Check your tire pressure frequently during the winter. Cold temperatures make tire pressure go down. For every ten-degree drop in temperature, tire pressure will drop a pound. Correct pressure will give you the best handling, best stopping, and best wear of the tire.

Kitty Car

Carry a bag of kitty litter or sand in your trunk to provide traction in slippery spots.

Frigid Fluid

Check your car's oil as winter approaches. In colder temperatures, some cars need a thinner oil. Read your owner's manual to find the recommended weight. Also make sure your car's coolant system is clean and full of fluid.

Overnight Ice

To prevent keyholes from freezing overnight, put a magnet over them. In the morning, remove the ice-covered magnet and the keyhole will be ice-free. Reduce your scraping on cold winter mornings by putting a large piece of cardboard or a blanket over your car's windshield the night before.

Carpet Keeper

Save your car's carpet from the seasonal abuse of heavy boots, snow, and slush by covering your floor with old towels.

Motor-Head of the Class

Take a basic car maintenance class at a community college. The knowledge and skill you gain will quickly pay for the class fee. If you can't take a class, look for other places to get low cost maintenance. Check with high school or trade school mechanic classes to see if they do repairs or maintenance on outside cars.

The repairs are done for teaching purposes, and many times you only pay for parts.

Mobile Phone

Keep a set of last year's phone books under your car seat. They are handy to look up an address or phone number while you're out and about. You will save gas by not driving around hunting for your destination.

Car Safety Kit

If you're stranded, provide safety and comfort with a home-made car safety kit. To make this kit cheaply, buy the contents below at garage sales and put them in a duffel bag or old suit-case:

- A dry change of clothes, including gloves, hat, and boots
- A sturdy tow rope
- Simple tools like a screwdriver and pliers
- Jumper cables
- Newspapers for insulation or starting a fire
- First aid supplies
- Electrical or duct tape
- Flares
- Bungee cord
- Chemical tire sealer
- Old blanket or sleeping bag
- Waterproof matches

To fashion a safety vest, buy a lightweight jacket at a garage sale. Pick one that's brightly colored and apply reflective tape to the back, front, and sleeves. Make your own "Need Help!" sign by printing your message on cardboard. Energy bars, bottled water, and a flashlight will need periodic replacement, but they're great to have too. Select items that will do double duty. The clothing in the kit can keep you warm, but if it is also bright red, it could be used as an emergency flag. An empty coffee can will hold the first aid kit or tools and can also be an emergency drinking cup.

Insurance

Shop around for the best insurance rates. Call the company that holds your homeowners' policy and ask for a discount if you insure your car with them too. If you have a good driving record, ask for a reduced rate. Young drivers cost more to have on a vehicle's policy, so save money by listing them as a part-time driver only. Students with good grades may also earn a lower rate. Discounts are available if you carpool, are a senior citizen or nonsmoker, or drive limited miles. Suspend coverage on your car if it's not in use. Military families on temporary assignment overseas don't need insurance on a car that's just sitting in the garage.

VIN Is In

Make your car less attractive to thieves by etching your vehicle identification number (VIN) on the windows. It's more difficult to dispose of property that is identifiable, so crooks stay away. Our city police department offers free VIN window etching. If your city doesn't have such a program, contact your insurance company or glass companies. They may offer this service for free as well. Or do it yourself with a kit. Ask your insurance company if this theft deterrent will qualify you for a discounted rate.

Runaway Parts

Accidentally driving into curbs and potholes can separate you from your hubcaps. If you've ever lost a hubcap, you know they can be expensive to replace. Increase your chances of having a hubcap returned to you by writing your name and phone number on the inside of the hubcap with a permanent marker.

Most gas caps are now leashed to vehicles but if you should lose your gas cap, don't despair. Some people absentmindedly drive off from the gas station without their gas cap. The stations collect these and will offer them for free to their customers who need them. Just ask.

Busted

Traffic tickets are expensive mistakes. If you've received a ticket for a common moving violation, like speeding, you might avoid paying the hefty fine. Many cities allow a ticket to be dismissed if you attend a defensive driving class. The classes are offered on nights and weekends and can be very interesting. There is a fee to attend the class, but it's always far less than the cost of the fine. And many insurance companies will give you a discount, if you send them proof of your class attendance.

Take Your Time

Don't wait until your current vehicle gives up the ghost before researching your next vehicle purchase. Cars won't last forever; begin planning your purchase based on how long you expect your present vehicle to last. Size up the money you've saved for a car one year before you plan to make a purchase. Then look at makes, models, safety records, and fuel efficiency data. Research the places that will give you the best price. When the day comes to buy the car, you'll be confident and prepared. You'll avoid a panicked sense of urgency to replace a dead car.

New Car Buying

If you're sold on the idea of getting a new car, here are some ways to get more for your money. Do your homework. Select a make and model with proven reliability, lower depreciation rates, and a good repair record. Check *Consumer Reports* car reviews at your library to find this information. Consider buying a less expensive demo model or a model that's being discontinued. Skip the bells and whistles like sports packages and power everything. Buy only what you really need. Know exactly what the dealer paid for the car before you buy it. This information is available at the library in *Edmund's New Car Prices* or the *Consumer Guide Auto Series*. Armed with this knowledge, you can tell the car dealership exactly how much you're willing to pay. Pay only the dealer's cost plus a reasonable profit.

Never pay the inflated sticker price. Paying cash is also a great negotiating tool.

Used Car Buying

A new car depreciates drastically during the first two years of ownership. This discourages many frugalites from buying a new car. They prefer to buy a good used car instead. Before you go shopping for a used car, find out the *National Automobile Dealers Association* (NADA) or *Kelly Blue Book* values for the car you're looking for. These publications are available at the library and your bank or credit union. Buy from owners who have maintenance records. Ask the owner if you can have the vehicle inspected by your mechanic before you buy it. Don't be afraid to haggle on the price and offer to pay cash if this will lower the price.

Seize the Daewoo

Used cars can be a smart buy if you know where to find them. Look for a good vehicle at a police auction. Annually our city's police department sells all the impounded property, including cars. These cars are sold "as is." Some vehicles may be in mint condition and some may need repair. But if you're handy with tools, they're a great deal. You can also find bargains on used cars at your bank. They receive repossessed vehicles frequently and auction them or sell them directly.

Senior Savings

When older drivers move to retirement centers, they often want to sell their car. Contact your nearest retirement home and let them know you are in the market for a good used car. Post your name and phone number on the center's bulletin board so new residents will be aware of your quest.

Donating a Car

When you replace your old clunker with a newer vehicle, consider donating your old car to charity. You no longer have the maintenance costs of your old car, and you get a tax write-off. Donating a car is quick and painless. Contact the charity's auto donations director and ask what documents to bring. After filling out a simple form, you'll sign over the title and receive a receipt. Make sure the car title is clearly signed over to the charity. If this transaction isn't done successfully, you could still be responsible for the car's taxes, registration, and inspection. Donate your car right before these costs are due to avoid paying them for the year.

8▲

"It goes without saying that you should never have more children than you have car windows."
—Erma Bombeck

Credit Cards: The Good, the Bad, and the Ugly

Before I (Deana) was married, I often "charged" my way through life. I thought nothing of putting even the most trivial item on my credit card. Since I foolishly spent more than I made, I was stuck making only the minimum payments. But in November 1985, I became engaged to Joe, a handsome and naturally frugal man. I thought the greatest thing I could give him would be a debt-free bride. So I determined to pay off my charge cards. It took me several months, but on Valentine's Day I handed him a heart-shaped box filled with my paid-off cards, cut into pieces. Nothing says "I love you!" like tiny pieces of plastic.

Many people charge their way through life as I did. The average U.S. household has credit card balances totaling over $5,000. Nationally, installment debt has reached $1.2 trillion.

Our culture is accustomed to an economy of credit and debt. Credit cards are a big part of that culture. Credit cards are useful to make purchases over the telephone and internet. They serve as identification and are handy in an emergency. They help us establish a credit history, which is useful when seeking a loan. But there are ways to reduce our dependence on credit cards and the interest we pay each year.

Stop on a Dime

Stop spending. It sounds simplistic but you cannot get out of debt if you continue to incur more debt. You also can't build up savings if every extra penny is going to service your credit card debt. Declare a moratorium on all new purchases.

Close Out

Reduce your spending by closing as many accounts as you can, such as individual store accounts and gas company accounts. Immediately destroy any new unsolicited credit cards you receive. You should keep only one or two major bank credit cards (Visa, MasterCard) for emergencies only.

Cold Cash

A practical way of limiting credit card use is to freeze your card—literally. Put your major credit cards in a container of water and pop it in the freezer. Should an emergency occur it is still available, but it is inconvenient enough to keep you from impulse purchases and daily use. This will require you to operate with cash only. The sight of money vanishing from your wallet will alert you to how much you're spending.

Show Me the Money

Face up to the debt you already have. Total up what you owe on store cards, gas cards, bank cards, and layaways. This can be difficult—and scary. Amazingly, many otherwise intelligent people fearfully hide their heads in the sand when it comes to credit cards. They unfortunately choose financial illiteracy over financial knowledge. Calculate how much you owe, to whom, and at what interest rate. Write it down! Knowledge is power and once you know your financial standing you can begin to make positive changes.

Dear Diary

Folks who don't know what they owe probably don't know what they're spending. Create a spending diary. Record every penny you spend for one month. If this task is too overwhelming, use your checkbook and credit card statements as your diary. But remember cash expenditures will not be listed on these records. A diary will show you where your money's going and help you find places to cut back.

Get a Plan

Gather the family around the kitchen table and make a plan to get out of credit card debt. This plan should contain ideas for limiting your current spending and applying the money saved to your current debt. Ask for everyone's input. Changes in lifestyle, like eating out less or cutting off cable TV, will be easier to accept if everyone participates.

Pick a Card, Any Card

Most experts recommend that every spare dime be applied to the credit card bill that is charging the highest interest rate, not just the biggest bill. By paying this one off first, you'll save the most in interest charges. However, some advisers recommend paying off a small balance first. The sense of accomplishment you receive will motivate you to continue your anti-debt pursuit.

Maximum Minimum

Don't pay just the minimum payment. According to Consumer Credit Counseling Services, paying the $60 minimum payment on a $3,000 credit card balance would take eight years to pay off and cost a whopping $2,780 in interest! By adding an additional $50 a month, the debt could be paid off in three years and spare you $1,800 in interest charges. As you begin to shrink the total amount owed, the minimum payment will go down also. But don't be tempted to lessen the amount you're paying. Keep putting as much into it as possible.

Rapid Debt Repayment

When you finish paying off the first balance, you may be tempted to take your new financial freedom and spend it. Don't do it. Instead, take the money you've been using for debt repayment, add a little more to it, and start on the next balance. This is known as Rapid Debt Repayment. When all your debt is eliminated you will be free to take the money you had been putting toward debt and begin to meet other financial goals.

Rate Seeking

Know the interest rate the bank is charging you. If you have a large balance on a high-interest card, you can transfer that balance to an introductory or teaser rate card that has lower interest charges. This will save you money on the amount of interest you're paying. Be aware that the teaser rate will only last a few months before it jumps to a much higher rate. Pay off the balance before the rate spike. Some people leapfrog their balances from one teaser card to another. But this activity will show up on your credit report as a sign of instability.

Know Your Limits

Having several cards with high credit limits can restrict your ability to get a loan. Banks view your credit limits as potential debt. Even if your cards are not maxed out and you pay your balances on time, too much unused credit is a stumbling block to loan approval. Close out unused accounts or contact your credit card company and ask them to lower your credit limit.

Fees

Shop around to find a credit card with no annual fee. This will save you as much as $50 a year. We have a no-fee Visa through our credit union. Always make a monthly payment on time. If you are just one day late, you can be slapped with a late fee of up to $30. If you are late paying twice, you may be forced to pay a penalty interest rate, as much as 26 percent.

Checks and Balances

Many people make the mistake of paying their credit card bill without reading it thoroughly. Keep the receipts from your credit card purchases in an envelope labeled with the month the purchase was made. When your credit card statement arrives, compare the receipts to the purchases listed on the statement. Call the credit card company immediately if you find an overcharge or a duplicate charge. Also review your statement for any extra charges or fees. You may be paying for unnecessary services, like credit card insurance, without realizing it.

Affinity Cards

Affinity credit cards offer a reward, such as airline miles, for using the card. For every dollar you charge on these cards you get one frequent flier mile. Many people love these cards and know how to make them work for them. In order for an affinity card to benefit you, follow these guidelines.

Select a card that offers miles on an airline with regular service to your nearest airport. It doesn't make sense to earn miles with an airline that has only a few flights to your area. Choose a card with a lower annual fee. Affinity cards charge anywhere from $50–$100. Pay off your balance each month. Frequent flier miles are not worth debt and interest rates.

Do the math. In order to earn one round-trip ticket, you must accumulate $25,000 in charges. If you charge at least $8,333 each year for three years, you would earn one ticket. Assuming you always paid off your balances and your annual fee was $50, you would have paid $150 for the "free" ticket. If you redeem the ticket for a flight worth $250, then you've saved $100 on your travel expenses.

In order to earn miles faster, many people put all their purchases on affinity cards. This is wise only if you control your financial impulses and are prepared to pay off the balance each month.

❧

"Live within your income. Always have something saved at the end of the year. Let your imports be more than your exports, and you'll never go far wrong."
—*Samuel Johnson*

INDEX

Visit our website at www.frugalfamilynetwork.com

Now Available from Frugal Family Network,® Inc.

If you enjoyed the book, you'll love other products from the Frugal Family Network.

Frugal Family Network Newsletter: The newsletter is a fun and practical guide to thrifty living. Each issue contains timely money saving tips to help you live better and pay less! Regular features include: cooking tips, healthy and cheap recipes, recycling, ideas for kids, gifts, and much more. Order today to learn the old fashioned money sense that helps Frugal Friends Angie and Deana get the most out of every penny. It also makes a great gift! Eight pages/issue, 6 issues/year, $12 US, $14 Canada.

"Winning the Grocery Store Battle" Audio Tape: Be a winner at the checkout stand! The Frugal Family Network will teach you how to cut your food budget more than you ever thought possible. Angie reduced her average monthly food bill from $400/mo. for her family of four to an amazing $135/mo. Deana's grocery spending dropped from $380/mo. to $180/mo. On this 60-minute live workshop recording you'll learn to spot the supermarket deals and avoid the money traps, while providing healthy meals for your family. Only $6 each.

Frugal Family Network Order Form

Name _____

Address _____

City_____State/Prov_____ ZIP/Postal Code_____

Phone_____Email_____

Please send me: Qty.
Frugal Family Network Newsletter Subscription(s)   ____@ $12 ea. = $_____
 "Winning the Grocery Store Battle" Workshop Audio Tape   ____@ $6 ea. = $_____
Canadian orders: add $2 shipping & handling per item ordered ____@ $2 ea. = $_____
Outside of the US or Canada: add $4 shipping per item   ____@ $4 ea. = $_____
                                                              Total = $_____

Canadian and Intl. *orders:* Please send US funds only in International or Postal Money Orders.

Mail to:
Frugal Family Network, Inc.
PO Box 92731
Austin, TX 78709

POPULAR BOOKS BY STARBURST PUBLISHERS®

Cheap Talk with the Frugal Friends
By Angie Zalewski and Deana Ricks
A collection of savvy tips and tricks for stretching the family dollar from the celebrity thrifters known as the Frugal Friends by their radio and television audiences.
(trade paper) ISBN 1892016583 **$9.99**

A Growing Heart: Stories, Lessons, and Exercises Inspired by Proverbs
Edited by Kathy Collard Miller
The profound truths of Proverbs provide wisdom for making good choices in life. Each selection includes a verse from Proverbs, an inspirational story, teaching, quotation, and idea for journaling with room to write.
(trade paper) ISBN 1892016524 **$12.99**

Also available:
An Expressive Heart: Stories, Lessons, and Exercises Inspired by the Psalms
(trade paper) ISBN 1892016508 **$12.99**

Bible Seeds: A Simple Study-Devotional for Growing in God's Word
From the creators of the God's Word for the Biblically-Inept™ series
Growing your faith is like tending a garden—just plant the seed of God's Word in your heart, tend it with prayer, and watch it blossom. At the heart of this unique study is a Bible verse or "seed" that is combined with an inspirational lesson, a word study, application tips, thought questions with room to write, a prayer starter, and a final thought.
(trade paper) ISBN 1892016443 **$13.99**

God Things Come in Small Packages: Celebrating the Little Things in Life
By Susan Duke, LeAnn Weiss, Caron Loveless, and Judith Carden
Enjoy touching reminders of God's simple yet generous gifts to brighten our days and gladden our hearts! Treasures like a sunset over a vast, sparkling ocean; a child's trust; or the crystalline dew on a spider's web come to life in this elegant compilation.
(cloth) ISBN 1892016281 **$12.95**

What's in the Bible for . . .™ Women
By Georgia Curtis Ling
What does the Bible have to say to women? Women of all ages will find biblical insight on topics that are meaningful to them in four sections: Wisdom for the Journey; Family Ties; Bread, Breadwinners, and Bread Makers; and Fellowship and Community Involvement.
(trade paper) ISBN 1892016109 **$16.95**

Don't Miss These Popular Websites!
www.biblicallyinept.com
www.sundayschoolteach.com
www.homeschoolteach.com
www.learntheword.com

Purchasing Information
www.starburstpublishers.com

Books are available from your favorite bookstore, either from current stock or special order. To assist bookstores in locating your selection, be sure to give title, author, and ISBN. If unable to purchase from a bookstore, you may order direct from STARBURST PUBLISHERS. When ordering please enclose full payment plus shipping and handling as follows:

Post Office (4th class)
$4.00 with purchase of up to $20.00
$5.00 ($20.01–$50.00)
9% of purchase price for purchases of $50.01 and up

Canada
$5.00 (up to $35.00)
15% ($35.01 and up)

United Parcel Service (UPS)
$5.00 (up to $20.00)
$7.00 ($20.01–$50.00)
12% ($50.01 and up)

Overseas
$5.00 (up to $25.00)
20% ($25.01 and up)

Payment in U.S. funds only. Please allow two to four weeks minimum for delivery by USPS (longer for overseas and Canada). Allow two to seven working days for delivery by UPS. Make checks payable to and mail to:

Starburst Publishers®
P.O. Box 4123
Lancaster, PA 17604

Credit card orders may be placed by calling 1-800-441-1456, Mon.–Fri., 8:30 A.M. to 5:30 P.M. Eastern Standard Time. Prices are subject to change without notice. Catalogs are available for a 9 x 12 self-addressed envelope with four first-class stamps.